THE SECRET OF A
HAPPY HOME

I0617698

MARION HARLAND

1st WORLD
LIBRARY
Literary Society

The Secret of a Happy Home

Marion Harland

© 1st World Library, 2007
PO Box 2211
Fairfield, IA 52556
www.1stworldlibrary.com
First Edition

LCCN: 2007901830

Softcover ISBN: 978-1-4218-4302-5
Hardcover ISBN: 978-1-4218-4204-2
eBook ISBN: 978-1-4218-4400-8

Purchase *"The Secret of a Happy Home"*
as a traditional bound book at:
www.1stWorldLibrary.com/purchase.asp?ISBN=978-1-4218-4302-5

1st World Library is a literary, educational organization
dedicated to:

- Creating a free internet library of downloadable ebooks

- Hosting writing competitions and offering book
publishing scholarships.

Interested in more 1st World Library books?
contact: literacy@1stworldlibrary.com
Check us out at: www.1stworldlibrary.com

1st World Library Literary Society

Giving Back to the World

"If you want to work on the core problem, it's early school literacy."

- James Barksdale, former CEO of Netscape

"No skill is more crucial to the future of a child, or to a democratic and prosperous society, than literacy."

- Los Angeles Times

Literacy... means far more than learning how to read and write... The aim is to transmit... knowledge and promote social participation."

- UNESCO

"Literacy is not a luxury, it is a right and a responsibility. If our world is to meet the challenges of the twenty-first century we must harness the energy and creativity of all our citizens."

- President Bill Clinton

"Parents should be encouraged to read to their children, and teachers should be equipped with all available techniques for teaching literacy, so the varying needs and capacities of individual kids can be taken into account."

- Hugh Mackay

DEDICATION

To My Children,
"The Blessed Three,"
Whose Love and Loyalty
Have made mine a Happy Home
And my Life Worth Living,
The volume is
Gratefully Dedicated.

MARION HARLAND

CONTENTS

INTRODUCTORY

AN OPEN SECRET

Some one asked me the other day, if I were not "weary of being so often put forward to talk of 'How to Make Home Happy,' a subject upon which nothing new could be said."

My answer was then what it is now: Were I to undertake to utter one-thousandth part that the importance of the theme demands, the contest would be between me and Time. I should need "all the time there is."

Henry Ward Beecher once prefaced a lecture delivered during the Civil War by saying: "The Copperhead species chancing to abound in this locality, I have been requested to select as my subject this evening something that will not be likely to lead to the mention of Slavery."

"I confess myself to be somewhat perplexed by this petition," the orator went on to say, with the twinkle in his eye we all recollect—"for I have yet to learn of any subject that could not easily lead me up to the discussion of a sin against God and man which I could not exaggerate were every letter a Mt. Sinai—I mean, American Slavery."

Likening the lesser to the greater, allow me to say that I cannot imagine any topic worthy the attention of

God-fearing, humanity-loving men and women that would not be connected in some degree, near or remote, with "Home, and How to Make Home Happy."

The general principles underlying home-making of the right kind are as well-known as the fact that what is named gravitation draws falling bodies to the earth. These principles may be set down roughly as Order, Kindness and Mutual Forbearance. Upon one or another of these pegs hangs everything which enters into the comfort and pleasure of the household, taken collectively and individually. They are the beams, the uprights and the roofing of the building.

The chats, more or less confidential and altogether unconventional, which I propose to hold with the readers of this modest volume have to do with certain sub-laws which are so often overlooked that—to return to the figure of the building—the wind finds its way through chinks; the floors creak and the general impression is that of bare homeliness. House and Home go together upon tongue and upon pen as naturally as hook-and-eye, shovel-and-tongs, knife-and-fork,—yet the coupling is rather a trick learned through habit than an act of reason. The words are not synonyms of necessity or in fact.

Upon these, the first pages of my unconventional book, I avow my knowledge of what, so far from humiliating, stimulates me—to wit, that nine-tenths of those who will look beyond the title-page will be women. This is well, and as I would have it to be, for without feminine agency no house, however well appointed, can be anything higher than an official residence.

Man's first possession in a world then unmarred by sin was a dwelling-place—but Eden was not a home until the woman joined him there. Throughout the ages and all over the world, as mother, wife, sister, daughter (often, let me

Marion Harland

observe in passing, as old-maid aunt) she has stood with him as the representative of the rest, sympathy and love to be found nowhere except under his own roof-tree, and beside his own fireside. It is not the house that makes the home, any more than it is the jeweled case that makes the watch, or the body that makes the human being. It is the Presence, the nameless influence which is the earliest acknowledged by the child, and the latest to be forgotten by man or woman. The establishment of this power is essentially woman's prerogative.

In this one respect—I dare not say in any other—we outrank our brothers. They can build palaces and the furniture that fits them up in regal state; they can, even better than we, prepare for the royal tables food convenient for them, and fashion the attire of the revelers, and make the music and sing the songs and write the books and paint the pictures of the world. They may make and execute our laws and sail our seas, and fight our battles, and—after dutiful consultation with us—cast our votes. There is no magnanimity in admitting all this. It is the due of that noblest work of God, a strong, good, gentle man to receive the concession and to know how frankly we make it. To them as theologians, logicians, impartial historians, as priests, prophets, and kings—we do cheerful obeisance, yet with the look of one who but half hides a happy secret in her heart that compensates for all she resigns. There is not a true-hearted woman alive who would give up her birthright to become—we will say Christopher Columbus himself.

It must be a fine thing, though, to be a man on some accounts;—to be emancipated forever-and-a-day from the thraldom of skirts for instance, and to push through a crowd to read the interjectional headlines upon a bulletin board, instead of going meekly and unenlightened home, to be told by John three hours later that "a woman's curiosity passes masculine comprehension, and that he is too tired and hungry to talk." It must be a satisfaction to be able to hit another nail with a hammer than that attached to one's own thumb, and to hurl a stone from the shoulder instead of tossing it from the wrist; there must be sublimity in the thrill with which the stroke-oar of the 'Varsity's crew bends to his work, and the ecstasy of the successful crack pitcher of a baseball team passes the descriptive power of a woman's tongue. Nevertheless, the greatest architectural genius who ever astonished the world with a pyramid, a cathedral, or a triumphal street-arch, could never create and keep a Home. The meanest hut in the Jersey meadows, the doorway of which frames in the dusk of evening the figure of a woman with a baby in her arms, silhouetted upon the red background of fire and lamp kindled to welcome the returning husband and father, harbors as guest a viewless but "incomparable sweet" angel that never visits the superb club-house where men go from spirit to spirit in the vain attempt to make home of that which is no home.

"You write—do you?" snarled Napoleon I, insolently to the wittiest woman of the Paris salons. "What, for instance, have been some of your works since you have been in this country?"

"Three children, sire!" retorted the mother of Madame Emile de Girardin.

It was this same ready witted mother whom another woman pronounced the happiest of mortals.

"She does everything well—children, books and preserves."

Her range was wide. Comparatively few of her sex can grasp that octave. Upon the simplest, as upon the wisest, Heaven has bestowed the talent of home-making, precious and incommunicable.

Woman's Work in the Home! Taking up, without irreverence, the magnificent hyperbole of the beloved disciple, I may truly say, "that if they should be written, every one, I suppose the world itself would not contain the books that would be written."

Let us touch one or two points very briefly. I have said that men can furnish houses more artistically than we, and that as professional cooks they surpass us. It should follow naturally that men, to whose hearts the stomach is the shortest thoroughfare, would, in a body, resort to hotels for daily food. There is but one satisfactory explanation of the unphilosophical fact that the substantial citizen who, during a domestic interregnum, makes the experiment of three meals a day for one month at the best restaurant in New York City (and there are no better anywhere) returns with gladness and singleness of heart to his own extension-table—and that were I to put the question "Contract Cookery or Home Cookery?" to the few Johns who deign to peruse these lines, the acclaim would be—"Better, as everyday fare, is a broiled beefsteak and a mealy potato at home, than a palatial hotel and ten courses."

There is individuality in the steak broiled for John's very self, and sentiment in the pains taken to keep the starch in his potato, and solid satisfaction in putting one's knees under his own mahogany. The least romantic of gourmands objects to stirring his appetite into a common vat with five hundred others. But there is something back of all this that makes home-fare delicious, when the house mother smiles across the dish she has sweetened with love and spiced with good-will, and thus transformed it into a message from her heart to the hearts of the dear ones to whom she ministers.

John—being of the masculine gender according to a decree of Nature, and, therefore, irresponsible for the slow pace at which his wits move—may not be able at once to analyze the odd heartache he feels in surveying the apartments fitted up by the upholsterer—or to tell you why they become no longer a tri-syllabled word, but "our rooms," within a day after wife and daughters have taken possession of them. The honest fellow cannot see but that the furniture is the same, and each article standing in the same place—but the new atmosphere "which is the old," greets him upon the threshold, and steals into his heart before he has fairly entered. Anybody could have shaken the stiffness out of that portiere, and put a low, shaded lamp under the picture he likes best, and broken up the formal symmetry of the bric-a-brac that reminded him, although he did not dare confess it, of a china shop, and set a slender vaselet with one big ragged golden globe of a chrysanthemum in it here, and over there a bowl of long-stemmed roses—(his favorite Bon Silenes, too). But what hireling, O blind and dear John! would have left a bit of fancy work with the needle sticking in it, and scissors lying upon it, on the table in library or smoking room, and put the song you always ask for at twilight upon the open piano, and, just where you would choose to cast yourself down to listen, your especial Sleepy Hollow of chair or lounge with the slumber robe worked last Christmas by loving fingers thrown invitingly across it?

What professional art could make the vestibule of your house—a rented cottage, maybe—the gateway to another, and a purer, higher, happier sphere than the world you shut out with the closing of the front door? You would never get upon so much as bowing terms with your better self but for that front door and the latch key which lets you into the hall brightened by loving smiles, made merry by welcoming voices.

Talk of the prose of everyday life! When Poetry is hounded from every other nook of the earth which the Maker of it meant should be one vast, sublime epic, she will find an inviolable retreat under the Lares and Penates guarding the ingleside, and crown as priestess forever the wife and mother who makes and keeps the Home.

It could hardly be otherwise. To no other of his co-workers does the Lord of life grant such opportunities as to woman. Her baby is laid in the mother's arms to have, and to hold, and to fashion, without let or hindrance. His mind and heart are unwritten paper, and Nature and Providence unite in waving aside all who would interfere with what she chooses to inscribe thereupon. Her growing boys and girls believe in her with absoluteness no other friend will ever inspire—not in her love alone, but in her infallibility and her omnipotence. It is a moment of terror and often the turning point in a child's life, when first he comprehends that there are hurts his mother cannot heal, knowledge which he needs and she cannot impart.

If the boundaries of home seem sometimes to circumscribe a woman's sphere, they are also a safe barricade within which husband, and the children who have come to man's estate, find retreat from the outer storm and stress, a sanctuary where love feeds the flame upon the domestic altar. There, the atmosphere, like that of St. Peter's Church, never changes. It refreshes when the breath of the world is a simoon, withering heart and strength. When the winds of adversity are bleak, the shivering wanderer returns to the fold, "curtained and closed and warm—" to gather force for to-morrow's strain.

"Love, rest and home!"

we sing with moistened eyes. The blessed three are put in trust with woman. Other stations of honor and usefulness may be opened to her, but this is the realm of which nothing can dispossess her. The leaven that leavens the nations is wrought by her hands. Hers is the seedtime that determines what harvest the Master shall reap. To her is committed the holy task of preserving all that we can know of a lost paradise until we see the light flash out for our eager eyes from the wide doors of what—when we would draw it nearest and make it dearest to our hearts—we call our Changeless Home.

CHAPTER I

SISTERLY DISCOURSE WITH JOHN'S WIFE CONCERNING JOHN

John is not John until he is married. He assumes the sobriquet at the altar as truly as his bride takes the title of "Mistress" or "Madame." Once taken, the name is generic, inalienable and untransferable. Yet, as few men marry until they have attained legal majority, it follows that your John—my John—every wife's John—must have been in making for a term of years before he fell into our hands.

Sometimes he is marred in the making.

The most loyal wife admits to her inmost self in the most confidential season of self-communion, that she could have brought up her husband better than his mother or whatever feminine relative had the training of him succeeded in doing. An opinion which, I remark, is not shared by the relative in question. The mother of a growing son will know how to sympathize with her Mamma-in-law, when her own son—

"—will a-wooing go,
Whether his mother will or no."

I am John's advocate and best friend, but I cannot withhold

the admission that he has some grave faults, and one or two incurable disabilities. Grappling, forthwith, with the most obstinate of these last—I name it boldly. John is not—he never can be—and would not be if he could—a woman. Taking into consideration the incontrovertible truth that nobody but a woman ever understood another woman—the situation is serious enough. So desperate in fact, that every mother's daughter of the missionary sex is fired with zealous desire to mend it, and chooses for a subject her own special John—*in esse* or *in posse*.

This may sound like badinage, but it is uttered in sad earnest. The wife's irrational longing to extract absolute sympathy of taste, opinion and feeling, from her wedded lord, is a baneful growth which is as sure to spring up about the domestic hearth as pursley—named by the Indian, "the white man's foot"—to show itself about the squatter's door. Once rooted it is as hard to eradicate as plantain and red sorrel.

I brand it as "irrational," because common sense shows the extreme improbability that two people—born of different stocks, and brought up in different households—the man, sometimes, in no household at all—should each be the exact counterpart of the other; should come together provided respectively, with the very qualities, likes and dislikes, that the partner needs and prefers.

Add to the improbability aforesaid the inevitable variance of views upon divers important subjects consequent upon the standpoint masculine and the standpoint feminine, and the wonder grows—not that some marriages are unhappy, but that a large percentage of wedded couples jog on comfortably, and, if not without jar, without open scandal. That they do speaks volumes for the wisdom of Him who ordained marriage as man's best estate—and something— not volumes—perhaps, but a pamphlet or two—in behalf of

Marion Harland

human powers of philosophical endurance.

Before going farther it would be well to look our subject in the face—inspect it fairly and without prejudice pro or con.

Stand forth, honest John! and let us behold you, as God made and your mother—in blood, or in heart—trained you. Let the imagination of my readers survey him, as he plants himself before us. Albeit a trifle more conscious than a woman would be in like circumstances, of the leading fact that he has the full complement of hands and feet usually prescribed by Nature, he bears scrutiny bravely. He is what he would denominate in another, "a white man;" square in his dealings with his fellow-men and with a soft place, on the sunny side of his heart, for the women. He would add— "God bless them!" did we allow him to speak. Men of his sort rarely think of their own womenkind or of pure, gentle womanhood in the abstract, without a benediction, mental or audible.

Our specimen, you will note, as he begins to feel at ease in the honorable pillory to which we have called him—puts his hands into his pockets. The gesture supplies us with the first clause of our illustrated lecture. Without his pockets John would be a cipher, and a decimal cipher at that. If some men were not all pocket they would never be Johns, for no Jill would be so demented as to "come tumbling after" them. I have seen a pocket marry off a hump-back, a twisted foot and sixty winters' fall of snow upon the head, while a pocketless Adonis sighed in vain for Beauty's glance. A full pocket balances an empty skull as a good heart cannot; a plethoric pocket overshadows monstrous vices.

But at his cleanly best, John's pockets are an integral part of his personality. He feels after his pocket instinctively while yet in what corresponds in the *genus homo* with the polywog state in batrachia. The incipient man begins to strut as soon as mamma puts pockets into his kilted skirt—a stride as prophetic as the strangled crow of the cockerel upon the lowest bar of the fence.

The direst penance Johnny can know is to have his pockets stitched up because he will keep his hands in them. To deny him the right is to do violence to natural laws. He is the born money-maker, bread-winner, provider—the *huesbonda* of our Anglo-Saxon ancestry—and the pocket is his heraldic symbol, his birthright.

The pocket question obtrudes itself at an alarmingly early period of married life—whoever may be the moneyed member of the new firm. When, as most frequently happens, this is John, the ultra-conscientious may think that he ought, prior to the wedding-day, to have hinted to his highland or lowland Mary, that he did not intend to throw unlimited gold into her apron every day. If he had touched this verity however remotely, she would not have married him. The man who speaks the straight-forward truth in such circumstances might as well put a knife to his throat, if love and life are synonyms.

Honest John, thrusting his hands well towards the bottom of his pockets, smiles sheepishly, yet knowingly, in listening to this "discourse." Courtship is one thing and marriage is another in his code. Mary's primal mistake is in assuming—(upon John's authority, I regret as his advocate to say), that the two states are one and the same. Moonlight vows and noonday action should, according to her theory, be in exact harmony. John does not deceive consciously. Wemmick's office tenets differed diametrically from those he held at Walworth where his aged parent toasted the muffins, and Miss. Skiffins made the tea. The mellow fervency of John's "With all my worldly goods I thee endow"—must be taken in a Pickwickian and Cupidian sense. Reason and experience sustain him in the belief that a tyro should learn a business before being put in charge of important interests. Mary is a tyro whose abilities and discretion he must test before—in the words of the old song—he

   "gives her the key of his chest,
   To get the gold at her request."

Most women take to married and home-life easily, because naturally. The shadow of the roof-tree, the wholesome restraint of household routine and the peaceful monotony of household tasks accord well with preconceived ideas and early education. John's liking for domesticity is usually an acquired taste, like that for olives and caviare, and to gain aptitude for the duties it involves, requires patience. He needs filing down and chinking, and rounding off, and sand-papering before he fits decorously into the chimney-corner. And when there, he sometimes does not "season straight." He was hewed across the grain, or the native grain ran awry, or there is a knot in the wood.

"Why were those newel posts oiled before they were set up?" I asked of a carpenter.

"T' keep 'em from checkin', to be sure."

"Checking?"

"Yes, ma'am. Goin' in shaller cracks all over, 's wood's apt to do without it's properly treated beforehand. Sometimes 'twould crack clean through ef 'twarnt for the ile."

In his new position John is apt "to go in shaller cracks all over," unless his feminine trainer has been judicious in the use of lubricants—assuasive and dissuasive. If handled aright by the owner he, to do him justice, rarely "cracks clean through."

"Checking" in this case signifies the lack of the small, sweet courtesies which are the peaceable fruits of the Gospel of Conventionality. Breeding, good or bad, environs the growing lad, as Wordsworth tells us heaven lies about us in our infancy. The boy whose mother allows him to lounge into her presence with his cap upon his head, whose sisters wink indulgently at his shirt sleeves in parlor and at table— will don his hat and doff his coat in his wife's sitting-room. Politeness, like gingerbread, is only excellent when home-made, and is not to be bought for money.

I wonder if John—disposed by nature and too often by education to hold such niceties of custom as trifles and cheap—suspects what a blow is dealt to his wife's ideals when he begins to show, either that he respects her less than of old, or that he is less truly a gentleman than his careful conservation of elegant proprieties during their courtship led her to imagine. It costs him but a second's thought and slight muscular exertion to lift his hat in kissing her on leaving home in the morning, and in returning at evening. It ought not to be an effort for him to rise to his feet when she enters the room, and to comport himself at her table and in her drawing-room as he would at the board and in the parlor of his neighbor's wife. Each of these slight civilities elevates her in her own and in others' eyes, and tends to give her her rightful place as queen of the home and of his heart. She may be maid-of-all-work in a modest establishment, worn and depressed by over-much drudgery, but in her husband's eyes she is the equal of any lady in the land. Her stove-burned face and print gown do not delude him as to her real position. Furthermore—and this hint is directed sidewise at our "model"—a sense of the incongruity between the fine courtesy of her husband's manner, and of slovenly attire upon the object of his attentions—would incite her to neatness and becomingness in dress. It is worth while to look well in the eyes of one who never for a moment forgets that he is a gentleman, and his wife a lady.

When John finds himself excusing this and that lapse from perfect breeding in his home life with the plea—"It is only my wife!" he needs to look narrowly at his grain and his seasoning. He is in danger of "checking."

Being a man—or I would better say—not being a woman—John is probably made up without domestic tact, and his wife must be on her guard to cover the deficiency. For example, if by some mortifying combination of mischances, a dish is scantily supplied, he helps it out lavishly, scrapes the bottom officiously, and with innocent barbarity calls your attention to the fact that it needs replenishing.

"I tried once to hold my husband back from the brink of social disaster," said one wife. "We sat opposite to one another at a dinner party where the conversation neared a topic that would be, I knew, extremely painful and embarrassing to our hostess. My John led the talk—all unaware of the peril—and when the next sentence would, I felt, be fatal, I pressed his foot under the table. What do you think that blessed innocent did? Winced visibly and sharply—stopped short in the middle of a word, and stared at me with pendulous jaw, and—while everybody looked at him for the next breath—said, resonantly—'*Jane! did you touch my foot?*'"

The incident is essentially John-esque. I am as positive as if I had called for a comparison of experience, that every wife who reads this could furnish a parallel sketch from life. The average John is impervious to glance or gesture. I know one who is a model husband in most respects, who, when a danger-signal is hung out from the other end of the table, draws general attention in diplomatic fashion thus—

"Halloo! I have no idea what I have done or said, now! but when Madame gives her three-cornered frown, I know there are reefs ahead, on the starboard or the larboard side, and

I'd better take my soundings."

Women are experts in this sort of telegraphy. From one of them, such an *expose* would mean downright malice, or mischief, and be understood as such. John's voiced bewilderment may be harmful, but it is as guileless as a baby's. It may be true that men are deceivers ever, in money or love affairs. In everyday home life, there is about the most sophisticated, a simplicity of thought and word, a transparency of motive, and, when vanity is played upon cunningly, a naive gullibility—that move us to wondering admiration. It, furthermore, I grieve to admit, furnishes manoeuvring wives with a ready instrument for the accomplishment of their designs.

For another fixed fact in the natural history of John is that, however kindly and intelligent and reasonable he may be— he needs, in double harness, to be cleverly managed, to be coaxed and petted up to what else would make him shy. If driven straight at it, the chances are forty-eight out of fifty that he will balk or bolt.

A stock story of my girlish days was of a careless, happy-go-lucky housewife, who, upon the arrival of unexpected guests, told her maid "not to bother about changing the cloth, but to set plates and dishes so as to humor the spots."

She is a thrifty, not a slovenly manager, who accommodates the trend of daily affairs to humor her John's peculiarities and foibles; who ploughs around stumps, and, instead of breaking the share in tough roots, *eases up*, and goes over them until they decay of themselves. In really good ground they leave the soil the richer for having suffered natural decomposition. If John is prone to savagery when hungry (and he usually is), our wise wife will wait until he has dined before broaching matters that may ruffle his spirit.

It is more than likely that he has the masculine bias toward wet-blanketism that tries sanguine women's souls more sorely than open opposition. Some Johns make it a point of manly duty to discourage at first hearing any plan that has originated with a woman. I am fond of John, but this idiosyncrasy cannot be ignored. Nor is it entirely explicable upon any principle known in feminine ethics, unless it be intended by Providence as a counterweight to the womanly proclivity to see but one side of a question when we are interested in carrying it to a vote. John is as positive that there are two sides to everything, as Columbus was that the Eastern Hemisphere must have something to balance it. When Mary looks to him for instant assent and earnest sympathy, he casts about for objections, and sets them in calm array. She may have demonstrated in a thousand instances her ability to judge and act for herself, and may preface her exposition of the case in hand by saying that she has given it mature deliberation. It never occurred to him until she mentioned it; he may have sincerest respect for her sense and prudence—the chances are, nevertheless, a thousand to one that he will begin his reply with—

"That is all very well, my dear—but you must reflect, that, etc., etc., et cetera"—each et cetera a dab of wet wool, taking out more and more stiffening and color, until the beautiful project hangs, a limp rag, on her hands, a forlorn wreck over which she could weep in self-pity.

This is one of the "spots" to be "humored." Wives there are, and not a few of them, sagacious and tender, who have learned the knack of insinuating a scheme upon husbandly attention until the logical spouses find themselves proposing —they believe of their own free will—the very designs born of their partner's brains. This is genius, and the practical application thereof is an art in itself. It may also be classified for John's admonition, as the natural reaction of ingenious wits against wet-blanketism. The funniest part of the transaction is that John never suspects the ruse, even at the hundredth repetition, and esteems himself, in dogged complacency, the author of his spouse's goodliest ideas.

Such a one dreads nothing more than the reputation of being ruled by his wife. The more hen-pecked he is, the less he knows it—and vice versa. "He jests at scars who never felt a wound." She who has her John well in hand has broken him in too thoroughly to allow him to resent the curb, or to play with the bit.

His intentions—so far as he knows them—are so good, he tries so steadfastly to please his wife—he is so often piteously perplexed—this big, burly, blundering, blind-folded, *blessed* John of ours—that our knowledge of his disabilities enwraps him in a mantle of affectionate charity. His efforts to master the delicate intricacy of his darling's mental and spiritual organization may be like the would-be careful hold of thumb and finger upon a butterfly's wing, but the pain he causes is inconceivable by him. The suspicion of hurt to the beautiful thing would break his heart. He could more easily lie down and die for her than sympathize intelligently in her vague, delicious dreams, the aspirations, half agony, half rapture, which she cannot convey to his comprehension—yet which she feels that he ought to share.

Ah! the pathos and the pity—sometimes the godlike patience of that silent side of our dear John! Mrs. Whitney, writing of Richard Hathaway, tells us enough of it to beget in us infinite tolerance.

"Everything takes hold away down where I can't reach or help," says the poor fellow of his sensitive, poetical wife. "She is all the time holding up her soul to me with a thorn in it."

"He did not know that that was poetry and pathos. It was a natural illustration out of his homely, gentle, compassionate life. He knew how to help dumb things in their hurts. His wife he could not help."

It reminds us of Ham Peggotty's tender adjustment upon his palm of the purse committed to him by Emily for fallen Martha.

"'Such a toy as it is!' apostrophized Ham, thoughtfully, looking on it. 'With, such a little money in it, Em'ly, my dear.'"

We are reminded more strongly of rough, gray boulders holding in their hearts the warmth of the sunshine for the comfortable growth of mosses that creep over and cling to and beautify them.

John is neither saint nor hero, except in Mary's fancy sketch of the Coming Man. He remonstrates against canonization strenuously—dissent that passes with the idealist for modesty, and enhances her admiration. She is oftener to blame for the disillusion than he. With the perverseness of feminine nature she construes strength into coarseness of fibre, slowness into brutal indifference. Until women get at the truth in this matter of self-deception, disappointment surely awaits upon awakening from Love's young dream.

The surest guard against the shock of broken ideals is to keep ever before the mind that men are not to be measured by feminine standards of perfection. Mary has as little perception of perspective as a Chinese landscape painter; she colors floridly and her drawing is out of line.

Put John in his proper place as regards distances, shadow and environment, and survey him in the cool white light of common sense. Unless he is a *poseur* of uncommon skill, he will appear best thus.

Conjugal quarrels are so constantly the theme of ridicule and the text of warnings to the unwedded that we lose sight of the plain truth that husbands and wives bicker no more than parents and children, brothers and sisters. In every community there are more blood-relations who do not speak to one another than divorced couples. Wars and fightings come upon us, not through matrimony so much as through the manifold infirmities of mortal nature. John, albeit not a woman, is a vertebrate human being, "with hands, organs, dimensions, senses, affections, passions. If you prick him he will bleed, if you tickle him he will laugh, if you poison him he will die." In the true marriage, he is the wife's other self—one lobe of her brain—one ventricle of her heart—the right hand to her left. This is the marriage the Lord hath made.

The occasional clash of opinions, the passing heat of temper, are but surface-gusts that do not stir the brooding love of hearts at rest in one another.

While John remains loyal to his wedded wife, forsaking all others and cleaving to her alone, the inventory of his faults should be a sealed book to her closest confidante, the carping discussion of his failings be prohibited by pride, affection and right taste. This leads me to offer one last tribute to our patient (and maybe bored) subject. He has as a rule, a nicer sense of honor in the matter of comment upon his wife's shortcomings and foibles than she exhibits with regard to his.

Set it down to gallantry, chivalry, pride—custom—what you will—but the truth sheds a lustre upon our John of which I mean he shall have the full advantage. Perhaps the noblest reticence belongs to the Silent Side of him. I hardly think it is because he has no yearning for sympathy, no need of counsel, when he reluctantly admits to himself that that upon which he has ventured most is, in some measure, a disappointment. Be this as it may, Mary may learn discretion from him—and the lesson conned should be forbearance with offensive peculiarities, and, what she names to her sore spirit, lack of appreciation. Given the conditions of his fidelity and devotion—and she may well "down on her knees and thank God fasting for a good man's love."

CHAPTER II

THE FAMILY PURSE

In the last chapter I touched, firmly, as became the importance of the subject, upon the pocket question in its bearing upon the happiness of home-life. The matter is too grave to be disposed of in half-a-dozen paragraphs. It shall have a chapter of its very own.

There are certain subjects upon which each of us is afraid to speak for fear of losing temper, and becoming vehement. This matter of "The Family Purse" is one of the few topics in all the range of theory and practice, concerning which I feel the necessity of putting on curb and bridle when I have to deal with it, and conscience urges just dealing with all parties.

I have set down elsewhere what I crave leave to repeat here and with deliberate emphasis.

If I were asked, "What, to the best of your belief, is the most prolific and general source of heart-burnings, contentions, harsh judgment, and secret unhappiness among respectable married people who keep up the show, even to themselves, of reciprocal affection?" my answer would not halt for an instant.

"The crying need of a mutual understanding with respect to the right ownership of the family income."

The example of the good old Friend, who, in giving his daughters in marriage, stipulated that each should be paid weekly, without asking for it, a certain share of her husband's income, is refreshing as indicating what one husband had learned by his own experience. It goes no further in the absence of proof that the sons-in-law kept the pledge imposed upon them as suitors, or that in keeping it, they did not cause their respective wives to wish themselves dead, and out of the way of gibe and grudge, every time the prescribed tax was doled out to them.

Nor do I admit the force of the implication made by a certain writer upon this topic, that the crookedness in the matter of family finances is "separation and hostility between the sexes, brought about by the advancement and equality of women." Wives in all ages and in all countries, have felt the painful injustice of virtual pauperism, and struggled vainly for freedom.

The growth toward emancipation in the case of most of them amounts merely to the liberty to groan in print and to cry aloud in women's convocations. If the yoke is easier upon the wifely neck in 1896 than it was in 1846, it is because women know more of business methods, and are more competent to the management of money than they knew fifty years ago, and some husbands, appreciating the change for the better, are willing to commit funds to their keeping. The disposition of fathers, brothers and husbands to regard the feminine portion of their families as lovely dead weights, was justified in a degree by the Lauras and Matildas, who clung like wet cotton-wool to the limbs of their natural protectors. Dependence was reckoned among womanly graces, and insisted upon as such in *Letters to Young Ladies, The Young Wife's Manual, A Father's Legacy to his Daughters*, and other valuable contributions to the family library of half a century ago. Julia, as betrothed, assured wooing Adolphus that absolute dependence, even for the bread she should eat, and breath she should draw, would be delight and privilege. Julia, as wife, fretted and plained and shook her "golden chains inlaid with down," when married Adolphus took her at her word.

It is surprising that both parties were so slow in finding out how false is the theory and how injurious the practice of the cling-and-twine-and-hang-upon school.

From my window as I write I see an object lesson that pertinently illustrates the actual state of affairs in many a home. At the root of a stately cedar, sprang up, twenty years ago, a shoot of that most hardy and beautiful of native creepers, the wild woodbine or American ivy. It crept steadily upward, laying hold of branch and twig, casting out, first, tendrils, then ropes, to make sure its hold—a thing of beauty all summer, a coat of many colors in autumn, until it reached the top of the tree. To-day, the only vestige of cedar-individuality that remains to sight, is in the trunk, the bare branches, stripped of all slight twigs, and at the extremity of one of these, a few tufts of evergreen verdure, that proclaim "This was a tree."

In the novels and poems that set forth the eternal fitness of the cling-twine-and-depend school, the vine is always feminine, the oak (or cedar?) masculine. Not one that I know of depicts the gradual strangling of the independent tree by the depending parasite.

Leaving the object-lesson to do its part, let us reason together calmly upon this vexed subject. When a man solemnly, in the sight of Heaven and human witnesses, endows his wife at the altar with his worldly goods, it is either a deed of gift, or an engagement to allow her to earn her living as honestly as he earns his, a pledge of an equal partnership in whatever he has or may acquire. That it is not an absolute gift is proved by his continued possession of his property and uncontrolled management of the same; furthermore, by his custom of bestowing upon his wife such sums, and at such periods as best suit his convenience and pleasure—and by his expectation that she will be properly grateful for lodging, board and raiment. If he be liberal, her gratitude rises proportionably. If he be a churl, she must submit with Christian resignation.

The gossips at a noted watering-place where I once spent a summer, found infinite amusement in the ways of a married heiress, whose fortune was settled so securely upon herself by her father that her husband could not touch the bulk of it with, or without her consent. Her spouse was an ease-loving man of fashion, and accommodated himself grace-fully to this order of things. She loved him better than she loved her money, for she "kept" him well and grudged him nothing. It was in accordance with her wishes that he made no pretence of business or profession. "Why should he when she had enough for both?" she urged, amiably. His hand-some allowance was paid on the first of every month, and she exacted no account of expenditures. Yet she contrived to make him and herself the laughing stock of the place by her *naive* ignorance of the truth that the situation was peculiar. She sportively rated her lord in the hearing of others, for extravagance in dress, horses and other entertainments; affected to rail at the expense of "keeping a husband," and, now and then, playfully threatened to "cut off supplies" if he did not do this or that. In short, with unintentional satire, she copied to the letter the speech and tone of the average husband to his dependent wife.

"Only that and nothing more." Her purse-pride was obvious, but as inoffensive as purse-pride can be. She lacked refinement, but she did not lack heart. She would have resented the imputation that she reduced her good-looking, well-clothed, well-fed, well-mounted "Charley" to a state of vassalage against which any man of spirit would have rebelled. He knew that he could have whatever it was within her power to bestow, to the half of her kingdom. Her complaints of his prodigality meant as little as her menace of retrenchment, and nobody comprehended this better than he. The owner of the money-bags is entitled by popular verdict to his or her jest. Her pretended railing was "clear fun."

The deeper and juster significance of the much derided clause of the marriage vow is the second I have offered. "Live and let live" is a motto that should begin, continue and be best exemplified at home. The wife either earns an honorable livelihood, or she is a licensed mendicant. The man who, after a careful estimate of the services rendered by her who keeps the house, manages his servants, or does the work of the servants he does not hire; who bears and brings up his children in comfort, respectability and happiness; who looks after his clothing and theirs; nurses him and them in illness, and makes the world lovely for him in health—does not consider that his wife has paid her way thus far, and is richly entitled to all he has given or will ever give her—is not fit to conduct any business upon business principles. If he be sensible and candid, let him decide what salary he can afford to pay this most useful of his employes —and pay it as a debt, and not a gratuity. The probability is that he will find that the sum justifies her in regarding herself as a partner in his craft or profession, with a fair amount of working-capital.

There is but one equitable and comfortable way of relieving the husband from the charge and the fact of injustice, and the wife from the sorer burden of conscious pauperism. She ought to have a stated allowance for household expenses, to be disbursed by herself and, if he will it, to be accounted for to the master of the house, and a smaller, but sure sum which is paid to her as her very own, which she may appropriate as she likes. He should no more "give" her money, than he makes a present of his weekly wages to the porter who sweeps his store, or to the superintendent of his factory. The feeling that their gloves, gowns, under-clothing—everything that they wear, and the very bread that keeps life in their bodies, are gifts of grace from the husbands they serve in love and honor, has worn hundreds of spirited women into their graves, and made venal hypocrites of thousands. The double-eagle laid in the palm of the woman whose home duties leave her no time for money-making, burns sometimes more hotly than the penny given to her who, for the first time, begs at the street-corner to keep herself from starving.

The strangest of anomalies that have birth in a condition of affairs which everybody has come to regard as altogether right and becoming, is that the wife whose handsome wedding portion has been absorbed by her husband's business is as dependent upon his favor for her "keep" as she who brought no dot. She does not even draw interest upon the money invested. Is it to be wondered at that caustic critics of human nature and inconsistencies catalogue marriage for the wife under the head of mendicancy? Would it not be phenomenal if women with eyes, and with brains behind the eyes, did not gird at the necessity of suing humbly for really what belongs to them?

I have known two, or at most three women, who averred that they "did not mind asking their husbands for money." Out of simple charity I preferred to believe that they were untruthful, to discounting their disrespect and delicacy to the extent implied by the assertion. Yet the street beggar gets used to plying his trade, and I may have been mistaken.

Let us not overlook another side of the question under

perplexed debate. The woman who considers herself defrauded by present privations and what seem to her needless economies, loses sight, sometimes, of what John keeps before him as the load-star of his existence and endeavor; to wit, that toil and economy are for the common weal. He is not a miser for his individual enrichment, nor does he plan with deliberate design for the shadowy second wife. It is not to be denied that No. 2 often lives like a queen upon the wealth which No. 1 helped to accumulate, and killed herself in so doing. But John does not look so far as this. Much scrimping and hoarding may engender a baser love of money for money's self. In the outset of the task, and usually for all time, he means that wife and children shall have the full benefit of what he has heaped up in the confident belief that he knows who will gather with him. Men take longer views in these matters than women. To "draw money out of the business" is a form of speech to a majority of wives. To him whose household expenses overrun what he considers the bounds of reason, this "drawing" means harder work and to less purpose for months to come; clipped wings of enterprise, and occasionally loss of credit. He who has married a reasonably intelligent woman cannot make her comprehend this too soon. If he can enlist her sympathies in his plans for earning independence and wealth, he has secured a valuable coadjutor. If he can show her that he is investing certain moneys which are due to her in ways approved by her, which will augment her private fortune, he will retain her confidence with her respect.

Each of us likes to own something in his or her own right. The custom and prejudice that, since the abolition of slavery, make wives the solitary exception to the rule that the "laborer is worthy of his hire," are unworthy of a progressive age. The idea that such having and holding will alienate a good woman from the husband who permits it, degrades the sex. He whose manliness suffers by comparison with a level-headed, clear-eyed wife capable of keeping her own bank account, makes apparent what a mistake she made when she married *him*.

CHAPTER III

THE PARABLE OF THE RICH WOMAN AND
THE FARMER'S WIFE

The rich woman was born and brought up in New York City; the farmer's wife in Indiana.

They were as far apart in education and social station as if they had belonged to different races and had lived in different hemispheres.

They were as near akin in circumstances and in suffering as if they had been twin sisters, and brought up under the same roof.

The husband of one wrote "Honorable" before his name, and reckoned his dollars by the million. He was, moreover, a man of imposing deportment, bland in manner and ornate in language. As riches increased he set his heart upon them and upon the good things that riches buy. He had four children, and he erected ("built" was too small a word) a palatial house in a fashionable street.

Each child had a suite of three rooms. Each apartment was elaborately decorated and furnished. The drawing-rooms were crowded with bric-a-brac and monuments of the upholsterer's ingenuity. It was a work of art and peril to

Marion Harland

dust them every day. He developed a taste for entertaining as time went on and honors thickened upon him, and he mistook, like most of his guild, ostentation for hospitality. Every dish at the banquets for which he became famous was a show piece. He swelled with honest pride in the perusal of a popular personal paragraph estimating the value of his silver and cut glass at $50,000.

The superintendent, part owner, and the slave of all this magnificence was his wife. She was her own housekeeper, and employed, besides the coachman, whose business was in the stables and upon his box, five servants. There were twenty-five rooms in the palatial house, giving to each servant five to be kept in the spick-and-span array demanded by the master's position and taste. As a matter of course something was neglected in every department, the instinct of self-preservation being innate and cultivated in Abigail, Phyllis and Gretchen, "Jeems" and "Chawls." Even more as a matter of course, the nominal mistress supplemented the deficiencies of her aids.

The house was as present and forceful a consciousness with her as his Dulcinea with David Copperfield at the period when the "sun shone Dora, and the birds sang Dora, and the south wind blew Dora, and the wild flowers were all Doras to a bud." No snail ever carried her abode upon her back more constantly than our poor rich woman the satin-lined, hot-aired and plate-windowed stone pile, with her. The lines that criss-crossed her forehead, and channeled her cheeks, and ran downward from the corners of her mouth, were hieroglyphics standing in the eyes of the initiated for the baleful legend—

"HOUSE AND HOUSEKEEPING."

When she drove abroad in her luxurious chariot, behind high-stepping bays, jingling with plated harness, or repaired in the season to seashore or mountain, she was striving feebly to push away the tons of splendid responsibility from her brain.

One day she gave over the futile attempt. Something crashed down upon and all around her, and everything except inconceivable misery of soul was a blank.

Expensive doctors diagnosed her case as nervous prostration. When she vanished from the eyes of her public, and a high-salaried housekeeper, a butler, a nursery governess and an extra Abigail took her place and did half her work in the satin-lined shell out of which she had crept, maimed and well-nigh murdered, it was announced that she was "under the care of a specialist at a retreat."

A retreat! Heaven save and pardon us for making such homes part and parcel and a necessity of our century and our land!

Our Rich Man's Wife never left it until she was borne forth into the securer refuge of the narrow house that needed none of her care-taking. Upon the low green thatch lies heavily the shadow of a mighty monument that, to the satirist's eye, has a family likeness to the stone pile which killed her.

The Farmer's Wife was born and bred among the prairies, out of sight of which she had traveled but once, and that on her wedding journey. She came back from the brief outing to take possession of "her own house"—prideful phrase to every young matron.

It was an eight-roomed farmstead, with no modern conveniences. That meant, that all the water used in the kitchen and dwelling had to be fetched from a well twenty feet away; that there was no drain or sink or furnace; that stationary tubs had not been heard of, and the washing was wrung by hand. The stalwart farmer "calculated to hire" in haying, harvesting, planting, plowing, threshing and killing times. Whatever might have been the wife's calculations, she toiled unaided, cooking, washing, ironing, scrubbing, sewing, churning, butter-making and "bringing up a family," single-handed, with never a creature to lift an ounce or do a stroke for her while she could stand upon her feet.

When she was laid upon her bed—an unusual occurrence, except when there was a fresh baby—a neighbor looked in twice a day to lend a hand, or Mrs. Gamp was engaged for a fortnight. It was not an unusual occurrence for the nominally convalescent mother to get dinner for six "men folks" with a three-weeks old baby upon her left arm.

Her husband was energetic and "forehanded," and without the slightest approach to intentional cruelty, looked to his wife to "keep up her end of the log." He tolerated no wastefulness, and expected to be well fed and comfortable; and comfort with this Yankee mother's son implied tidiness. To meet his view, as well as to satisfy her own conscience, his partner became a model manager, a woman of "faculty."

I saw her last year in the incurable ward of a madhouse. From sunrise until dark, except when forced to take her meals, she stood at one window and polished one pane with her apron, a plait like a trench between her puckered brows, her mouth pursed into an anguished knot, her hollow eyes drearily anxious—the saddest picture I ever beheld, most awfully sad because she was a type of a class.

Some men—and they are not all ignorant men—are beginning to be alarmed at the press of women into other— I had almost said any other—avenues of labor than that of housewifery. Eagerness to break up housekeeping and try boarding for a while, in order "to get rested out," is not confined to the incompetent and the indolent. Nor is it altogether the result of the national discontent with "the greatest plague of life"—servants.

American women, from high to low, keep house too hard because too ambitiously.

It is, furthermore, ambition without knowledge; hence, misdirected. We have the most indifferent domestic service in the world, but we employ, as a rule, too few servants, such as they are. It is considered altogether sensible and becoming for the mechanic's wife to do her own housework as a bride and as a matron of years. Unless her husband prospers rapidly she is accounted "shiftless" should she hire a washerwoman, while to "keep a girl" is extravagance, or a significant stride toward gentility. The wife of the English joiner or mason or small farmer, if brisk, notable and healthy, may dispense with the stated service of a maid of all work, but she calls in a charwoman on certain days, and is content to live as becomes the station of a housewife who must be her own domestic staff.

Here is the root of the difference. In a climate that keeps the pulses in full leap and the nerves tense, we call upon pride to lash on the quivering body and spirit to run the unrighteous race, the goal of which is to seem richer than we are, and make "smartness" (American smartness) cover the want of capital. Having created false standards of respectability, we crowd insane asylums and cemeteries in trying to live up to them.

The tradesman who begins to acknowledge the probability that he will become a rich citizen, and whose wife has "feelings" on the subject of living as her neighbors do, takes the conventional step toward asserting himself and gratifying her aspirations by moving into a bigger house than that which has satisfied him up to now, and furnishing it

Marion Harland

well—that is, smartly, according to the English acceptance of the word.

Silks and moquette harmonize as well as calico and ingrain once did. A three-story-and-a-half-with-a-high-stoop house, without a piano in the back parlor, and a long mirror between the front parlor windows, would be a forlorn contradiction of the genius of American progress. As flat a denial would be the endeavor to live without what an old lady once described to me as, a "pair of parlors." The stereotyped brace is senseless and ugly, but one of the necessaries of life to our ambitious housewife. She would scout as vulgar the homely cheerfulness of the middle-class Englishman's single "parlor" where the table is spread and the family receives visitors. Having saddled himself with a house too big for his family, and stocked the showrooms with plenishings so fine that the family are afraid to use them unless when there is company, the prudent citizen satisfies the economic side of him by making menials of wife and daughters without thought of the opposing circumstance that he has practically endorsed their intention to make fine ladies of themselves. Neither he nor the chief slave of her own gentility, the wife, who will maintain her reputation for "faculty" or perish in the attempt, has a suspicion that the strain to make meet the ends of frugality and pretension, is palpably and criminally absurd. By keeping up a certain appearance of affluence and fashion, they assume the obligation to employ servants enough to carry out the design, yet in nine hundred and ninety-nine times out of every thousand, they ignore the duty.

I admit without demur that, as American domestics go, they are a burden, an expense and a vexation. Notwithstanding all these drawbacks, she who will not risk them should not live in such a way that she must make use of such instruments or overwork herself physically and mentally.

The entire social and domestic system of American communities calls loudly for the reform of simplicity and congruity. We begin to build and are not able to finish. Our economics are false and mischievous, our aims are petty and low. The web of our daily living is not round and even-threaded. The homes which are constructed upon the foundations of deranged, dying and dead women, are a mockery of the holy name. Our houses should be planned and kept for those who are to live in them, not for those who tarry within the doors for a night or an hour. When housekeeping becomes an intolerable care there is sin somewhere and danger everywhere.

Marion Harland

CHAPTER IV

LITTLE THINGS THAT ARE TRIFLES

I feel that in writing a chapter upon ways and means I may seem to many readers to be going over an oft-traversed road. Of articles and treatises on the ever-vexing subject there is no end. The whole human creation or, at all events, a vast majority of it, groaneth and travaileth together in the agony of trying to spread a little substance over a vast surface,—in the desperate endeavor to make a little money go a very long way. Every few months we notice in a daily newspaper the offer of a money-prize for the best bill of fare for a company-dinner for six people, to be prepared upon a ludicrously-small allowance. The number of contestants for this prize proves, not only the general interest felt in the subject, but also testifies to the urgent need of the reward on the part of the various would-be winners. The probabilities are that few of these writers have the means to set forth such a dinner as they describe.

Books portraying the feasibility of "Comfortable living on seven hundred a year," or "How to keep house on a restricted income," are both helpful and pernicious. The prospective housewife buys them eagerly and devours them with avidity. She and John are boarding now, but are soon to have a home of their own, and after perusing their newly purchased volumes, they decide that their limited income will amply enable them to live in comfort although, perhaps, not in luxury. The tiny house or flat is rented, and they settle down, as Mrs. Whitney's Emery Anne would say, "to realize their geography," or, more properly speaking, to live their recently acquired knowledge, which is, in many points, very useful.

But—and here comes the mischief wrought by over-sanguine literature—the authors of these books leave too many things out of the question. The expenses of moving and the purchase of necessary furniture are, of course, omitted, but Mary finds to her chagrin that fuel—no slight item in any family,—and light,—also absolutely essential,—have not been taken into account. These make a big hole in the income which had seemed all-sufficient. It is expedient, also, occasionally, to have a woman in to do a day's cleaning, and the weekly wash is a bugbear which makes our young people shudder. The poor little housewife has many an anxious, tearful hour in striving to make both ends meet, while the most amiable husband cannot help wondering audibly "how it is they cannot live as cheaply as other people do."

In housekeeping, as in all else, one must learn the lesson for one's self. All the rules and theories in all the books and periodicals in the country are worth little compared with three months of personal experience. Happy is the young wife who has had some practice in housekeeping in her father's house before the heavier responsibility of a home of her own rests on her shoulders.

Let me remind our Mary, first of all, of the truth that there is no meanness in economy, and that—as I cannot repeat too often or too strongly—waste is vulgar. It is not the lady who scorns to save scraps of butter, who throws the few cold boiled potatoes left from dinner into the ash-barrel, and empties the teaspoonful of cream from the bottom of the pitcher into the kitchen sink. Your servant will not have the brains and foresight to detect in these seemingly useless articles factors which may aid materially in the construction of a delicacy, or "help out" to-morrow's breakfast or lunch. It is amazing to the mistress who is her own cook how long things last and how far they go. All the interest which a hired cook may take in her work does not impart the peculiar care which one feels for that which is one's own.

In this point the woman without a domestic has the advantage over the woman with a servant, and she with one maid-of-all-work is better off than she who keeps two. Every extra mouth counts, and the waste caused by each added Bridget or Gretchen is incalculable. The only redress which the housekeeper with a servant has, is constant vigilance and personal supervision, and even then she is the loser. At the South the servants are used to having provisions kept under lock and key. Each day the mistress deals out the requisite flour, butter, eggs, etc., and the cook is perfectly satisfied. Were a Northern housekeeper to adopt this system she would soon have the misery of engaging new servants. The Irish and Germans among us are not accustomed to such restrictions, and will not tolerate them.

To utilize the little "left-overs," then, Mary must make up her mind to do much of her own cooking. If she has a servant in the kitchen, she may frequently so exchange work with her that the preparation of dainty dishes will fall to her share. Norah may sweep the parlor, wipe up the hall floor, or wash the windows while her mistress is attending to cooking too delicate for the domestic's fingers. The servant may do what I call the heavy kitchen-work, such as preparing vegetables for cooking, chopping meat, peeling potatoes, etc., and she should always be allowed to wash pots, pans and kettles, after the cooking is done. But if the mistress will spend half an hour in the kitchen before each meal, John will soon discover that his food has a delicacy of flavor and is served with a daintiness imparted only by a professional French cook,—or a lady.

Another of the petty economies which is not belittling is the washing of one's own dining-room dishes. The money saved by this process is easily understood by the housewife whose cut-glass and egg-shell china are continually smashed to fragments by the hirelings whose own the fragiles are not. The china bill for one year of the woman with many servants assumes proportions so huge that she is actually afraid to let herself consider its enormity. And there are still more things broken of which she is never told until the day comes when this or that article is needed, and the answer to inquiry is:

"An' sure ma'am, such a thing aint niver been in this house sence iver I come into it."

And as there is no way of proving the falsity of this statement, one must submit.

As I have said before, dish-washing, as done by a lady, takes little time and labor, and may be a pleasant occupation. The laborer, not the labor, makes a thing common or refined. With an abundance of scalding hot water, a soap-shaker, mop, gloves with the tips cut off, clean and soft dish-towels, and delicate glass and china, dish-washing is in every sense of the word a lady's work. The mistress will do it in one-third of the time, with five times the thoroughness, and one-tenth as many breakages as will the average servant. And when the dishes are washed and the table is spread for the next meal with pure linen, glistening glass and shining silver—who dares say that the glow of housewifely pride and satisfaction does not more than compensate for the little time and trouble expended to produce the agreeable result?

I have said that every additional mouth counts in the sum of family expenses, and for this reason many housekeepers of moderate means neglect the duty of hospitality. Pardon me if I say that I think this is one of the economies which, if carried too far, is more honored in the breach than in the observance. I do not advocate, indeed I reprehend, pretentious entertaining, such as dances, parties, etc. But it impresses me that it is, to a certain extent, a mean spirit that counts the cost in asking a friend to stay to a repast, to spend a night or a week. It is your duty to have things so nice every day, and always, that you cannot be too much "put out" by an occasional guest. When you invite your friend to make you a visit, explain that you live quietly, and that he will find a warm welcome. Then give him just what you give John, and make no apologies. Above all, do not let him feel that any additional labor caused by his presence throws the whole course of the household machinery out of gear. Do not invite to your home those for whom you have to make so great a change in your daily life. If you keep house as a lady should, you need not fear to entertain anyone who is worthy to be your friend. It is no disgrace if your circumstances are such that you cannot afford to keep a staff of servants at your beck and call.

These suggestions are but hints as to daily management. First and foremost, Mary must learn to systematize her work. Method and management do wonders toward saving time and money. Some housewives are always in a hurry and their work is never done, while others with twice as much to do never seem flurried, and have time for writing, sewing and reading. The secret of the success of the latter class lies in that one golden word—METHOD.

I hope the young housekeepers to whom this talk is addressed will not consider such trifles as I have mentioned, degrading. It is the work laid before them and consequently cannot be mean. Such labor, when sweetened by the thought of what it all means, is ennobling. I know that

Keats tells us that:

"Love in a hut with water and a crust, Is—Love forgive us!—cinders, ashes, dust!"

If Love were really there, "cinders, ashes, dust" could not be, and the water and crust may, by our Mary's skillful treatment, be transformed into a refreshing beverage and an appetizing *entree*. My faith in the powers of John's wife is great, and if John be satisfied, and tells her that he has the best little love-mate and housekeeper in the world, can she complain?

CHAPTER V

A MISTAKE ON JOHN'S PART

It is not discreditable to the sex to assert that a man is first attracted marriage-ward by the desire of the eye. He falls in love, as a rule, because she who presently becomes the only woman in the universe to him is goodly to view, if not actually beautiful. Goodliness being largely contingent upon apparel, it follows that Mary dresses for John—up to the marriage-day. He who descries signs of slatternliness in his beloved prior to that date, may well be shocked to disillusionment. As a girl in a home where the mother takes upon herself the heaviest work, and spares her pretty daughter's hands and clothes all the soil and wear she can avert, Mary must be indolent or phenomenally indifferent to what occupies so much of other women's thoughts, if she do not always appear in her lover's presence neatly and—to the best of her ability—becomingly attired. She quickly acquaints herself with his taste in the matter of women's costumes, and adapts hers to it, wearing his favorite colors, giving preference to the gowns he has praised, and arranging her hair in the fashion he has chanced to admire in her hearing.

In the work-a-day world of matrimonial life, much of all this undergoes a change. Washington Irving lived and died a fastidious, unpractical bachelor, or he might have modified the sketch of "The Wife," the Mary who, after unpacking trunks, washing china, pots and kettles, putting closets to rights, laying carpets, hanging pictures, clearing away straw, sawdust, and what in that day corresponded with jute—dusting and shelving books—and performing the hundred other duties contingent upon sitting down in the modest cottage hired by her bankrupt husband,—got tea ready (presumably preparing potatoes for the same) picked a big mess of strawberries from a bed opportunely discovered in the garden, donned a white muslin robe and sat down to the piano to while away a lagging hour while awaiting her Leslie's return.

The John of our common-sensible age knows in his sober mind that his bride, in the effort to accomplish one-fourth as much, would equip herself in a brown gingham, tie a big apron before her, draw a pair of his discarded gloves with truncated fingers upon her hands, and be too tired at night to do more than boil the kettle for the cup of tea which he is more than likely to drink at the kitchen table, spread with a newspaper—the linen not having been yet dug out of the case in which "mother and the girls" packed it.

As the months wear on, Mary learns, if her spouse does not, that white muslin comes to grief so speedily in the course of even light housework, as to swell the laundry bills inordinately. The embroidered tea-gowns in which she used to array herself upon the rare occasions of her betrothed's morning calls, gather dust streaks upon skirts and the under sides of the sleeves, and, watch as she may, catch spots in the kitchen. She considers,—being lovingly determined to help, not hinder her mate,—that his purse must purchase new garments when her trousseau is worn out, and she saves her best clothes for "occasions." John, being her husband, is no longer an occasion. Dark prints and ginghams, simply made, and freshened up at meal-times by full white aprons, are serviceable, sensible, economical and significant of our dear Mary's practical wisdom. They are by so many degrees less becoming to her than the dainty apparel of loverly memory, that we do not wonder at the surprised discontent of the young husband.

Marriage has made no distinct change in his apparel. In his business a man must be decent, or he loses credit. In masculine ignorance of the immutable law that in dislodging dirt some must cling to the garments and person of the toiler, he sets down his wife's altered appearance to indifference to his happiness. She may have labored from an early breakfast to a late dinner to make his home comfortable and tasteful; into each of the dishes served up with secret pride for his consumption, may have gone a wealth of love and earnest desire that would have set up ten poets in sonnets and madrigals. Because her hands are roughened and her complexion muddied by her work, and—in the knowledge that dishes are to be washed and the table re-set for breakfast, and the kitchen cleared up after he has been regaled—she has slipped on a dark frock in which she was wont to receive him on rainy evenings—he falls into a brown and cynical study, which dishonors his wife only a little more than it disgraces himself and human nature. "Time was"—so runs his musing—"when she thought it worth her while to take pains to look pretty. That was when there was still a chance of a slip 'twixt the cup and the lip. She has me fast now, and anything is good enough for a husband."

Not one syllable of this chapter is penned for the woman who deserves an iota of censure like the above. It is a wife's duty to study to look well in her husband's eyes, always and in all circumstances. Her person should be scrupulously clean, her hair becomingly arranged, her working-gown as neat as she can keep it, and relieved before John comes in by clean collar or ruching and a smooth white apron. It is altogether possible for the woman who "does her own work" to be as "well set-up"—to borrow a sporting phrase from John—as her rich neighbor who can drag a train over Oriental rugs from the moment she rises to a late breakfast until she sweeps yards of brocade and velvet up the polished stairs after ball, dinner or theatre-party.

What I have to do with now is John's unreasonable desire that his wife should—as the help-meet of a man who has his own way to make in the world—dress as well as when she was the unmarried daughter of an elderly gentleman whose way was made. Every sensible girl married to a poor man comprehends, as one trait of wifely duty, that she must make her trousseau last and look well as long as she can. In the honorable dread of suggesting to him whose fortune she has elected to share, that when her handsome gowns are no longer wearable she must replace lace with cotton lawns, and silk with all-wool merino or serge, she devises excuses for sparing the costly fabrics—pretexts which, to his shame it is said, he is prone to misunderstand. If men such as he could guess at the repressed longings for the brave array of other times that assail the wearers of well-saved—therefore *passee*—finery, at sight of other women less conscientious, or with richer husbands than themselves, reveling in the latest and most enticing modes—if eyes scornful of plain attire could penetrate to the jealously locked closet where feminine vanity and native extravagance are kept under watch and ward by the love the critic is ready to doubt,—print, gingham and stuff gowns would be fairer than ermine and velvet in John's esteem.

CHAPTER VI

CHINK-FILLERS

At a recent conference of practical housewives and mothers held in a western city, one of the leaders told, as illustrative of the topic under discussion, an incident of her childhood. When a little girl of seven years, she stood by her father, looking at a new log-cabin.

"Papa," she observed, "it is all finished, isn't it?"

"No, my daughter, look again!"

The child studied the structure before her. The neatly hewed logs were in their proper places. The roof, and the rough chimney, were complete, but, on close scrutiny, one could see the daylight filtering through the interstices of the logs. It had yet to be "chinked."

When this anecdote was ended, a bright little woman arose and returned her thanks for the story, for, she said, she had come to the conclusion that she was one of the persons who had been put in the world to "fill up the chinks."

The chink-fillers are among the most useful members of society. The fact is patent of the founder of one of our great educational systems, that he grasped large plans and theories, but had no talent for minutiae. What would his majestic outlines be without the army of workers who, with a just comprehension of the importance of detail, fill in the chinks in the vast enterprise?

Putty may be a mean, cheap article, far inferior to the clear, transparent crystal pane, but what would become of the costly plate-glass were there no putty to fill in the grooves in which it rests, and to secure it against shocks?

The universal cry of the woman of the present to the effect that the sex has a mighty mission to accomplish, sounds a note of woe to her who, try as she may, can find no one occupation in which she excels and who feels that her only sphere in life is to go through the world doing the little things left undone by people with Missions. Does it ever occur to the self-named commonplace woman that her heaven-appointed task is as high a "mission" as any that may be taken up by her more gifted sisters?

It requires vast patience and much love for one's fellow-man to be a chink-filler. She it is who, as wife, mother, sister, or, perhaps, maiden-aunt, picks up the hat or gloves Mamie has carelessly left on the drawing-room table, wipes the tiny finger smears from the window-panes at which baby stood to wave his hand to papa this morning, dusts the rungs of the chair neglected by the parlor-maid, and mends the ripped coat which Johnny forgot to mention until it was nearly time to start for school. It is she who thinks to pull the basting-threads out of the newly finished gown, tacks ruching in neck and sleeves against the time when daughter or sister may want it in a hurry, remembers to prepare some dainty for that member of the household who is "not quite up to the mark" in appetite—in fact, undertakes those tasks, so many of which show for little when done, but which are painfully conspicuous when neglected. Does she bewail herself that her sphere is small—limited? Let her pause and consider how it would affect the family were the hat and gloves to be out of place, the chair undusted, the blurred window-glass overlooked, the coat unmended, the bastings allowed to stand in all their hideous white prominence, the invalid's appetite untempted. Like a good spirit, our chink-filler glides in and out among the fallen threads in the tangled web of life, picking up dropped stitches, fastening loose strands, and weaving the tissue into a harmonious whole, and yet doing it all so unobtrusively that the great weavers, looking only at the vast pattern they are forming, are unconscious that, but for the unselfish thought and deft fingers of the commonplace woman, their work would be a grand failure. Sometime the children whose shortcomings she has supplemented and thus saved from harsh reproof, the servants whose tasks she has made lighter, the husbands and wives, fathers and mothers, for whom she has made life smoother, and brighter, will arise and call her blessed. It may not be in this life, but it will surely come to pass in "the world that sets this right."

"She doth little kindnesses
Which most leave undone or despise;
For naught that sets one heart at ease,
Or giveth happiness or peace,
Is low-esteemed in her eyes."

Few people appreciate the dignity of detail, although, from the days of our childhood, we have heard rhymes, verses and proverbs innumerable which aim to impress mankind with the importance of the horse-shoe nail, of the rift in the lute, and the tiny worm-hole in the vessel through which the "watery tide" entered.

The wife and mother, more than any other, knows what a great part of life is made up of the little things, such as:—

"Sewing on the buttons,

Overseeing rations;
Soothing with a kind word
Guiding clumsy Bridgets,
Coaxing sullen cooks,
Entertaining company,
And reading recent books;
Woman's work!"

Strange as it may seem, the mind of the hireling cannot grasp the importance of the lesser tasks that go to make up the sum of existence. If you allow Bridget to prepare your guest chamber for an unexpected friend, you will observe that she glories in Rembrandt-like effects,—which, when viewed at a distance, assume a respectable appearance. You, with brains back of your hands, will notice that there is a tiny hole in the counterpane, dust under the table, and— above all—that the soap-dish is not clean. Your servant may do the rough work; the dainty, lady-like touch must be given by you.

You have an experienced waitress, and a jewel, if the dining-room and table are perfect without your supervision. It may be only that a teacup or plate is sticky or rough to the touch, a fork or a knife needed, the steel or one of the carvers forgotten. But when the family is assembled at the board, these trifles cause awkward pauses and interruptions.

Other little cares are to ascertain that the water with which the tea is made is boiling, that the alcohol lamp is filled, the flies brushed from the room, the plates warmed, and the sugar-dishes and salt-cellars filled. One housekeeper says that attention to these duties always reminds her of the task of washing one's face. Nobody notices if you keep your face clean, and you get no credit for doing it, but if you did not wash it, all the world would remark upon the dirt.

Often the work which "doesn't show" takes most time, and

tries the temper. And the hardest part of it all is that it is so frequently caused by others' laziness or delinquencies. If John would only use an ash-receiver, instead of strewing the veranda-floor with ashes and burnt matches; if he would "just think" to close the library blinds when he has finished looking for a missing book, instead of allowing the hot sunshine and flies to enter at their own sweet will, until, two hours after his departure for the office, you descend to the apartment which you had already dusted and darkened, and find it filled with heat and buzz! If that big boy of yours *could* remember to strip the covers from his bed when he arises and if your pretty daughter could cultivate her bump of order sufficiently to refrain from leaving a hat of some description in every room on the first floor, and her jacket on the banisters! Nobody but yourself knows how many precious minutes you expend in righting these wrongs caused by others' carelessness. John would advise grandly that you "Let Bridget attend to these matters. Why keep a dog and do your own barking?" If he is particularly sympathetic and generous, he will inform you seriously that your time is too precious to spend on beggarly trifles, and that if one servant cannot do the work of the establishment, he wants you to hire another. Perhaps you ungratefully retort that "it will only make one more for you to follow up and supplement."

It would be an excellent plan for each member of the household to resolve to put in its proper place everything which he or she observed out of order. By the time this rule had been established for twenty-four hours, the house would be immaculate, and the mother find ample time for her mission,—if she has any beside general chink-filler for the family. If not, she will have an opportunity to rest.

A well-known author, who is at the same time an exemplary housewife, tells of how she retired one rainy spring morning to her study in just the mood for writing. Husband and sons had gone to their various occupations. She had a splendid day for work ahead of her. She sat down to her desk and took up her pen. The plot of a story was forming itself in her brain. She dipped her pen in the ink and wrote:

"He was—"

A knock at the door. Enter Anne.

"Please, mem, a mouse has eat a hole in one of your handsome napkins,—them as I was to wash agin the company you're expectin' to-morrow night. By rights it should be mended before it's washed."

"Bring it to the sewing-room."

When the neat piece of darning was ended, the housekeeper repaired to the closet to put on a loose writing-sack. On the nail next to the jacket hung her winter coat. On the edge of the sleeve was a tiny hole. The housewifely spirit was filled with dread. There were actually *moths* in that closet! She must attend to it immediately. The woolens ought to be put up if moths had already appeared. John's clothes and the boys' winter coats were in great danger of being ruined. By lunch time the necessary brushing and doing up were ended. But in stowing away the winter garments in the attic, our heroine was appalled at the confusion among the trunks. The garret needed attention, and received it as soon as the noonday meal was dispatched. At four o'clock, with the waitress' assistance, the task was completed. About the same time a note arrived from John saying he would be obliged to bring two of his old friends—"swell bachelors"—who were spending the day in town, to dine with him that night. She "must not put herself to any trouble about dinner, and he would take them to the theatre in the evening." To the dinner already ordered were added oyster-pates, salad, with mayonnaise dressing, salted almonds, and, instead of the plain pudding that John liked, was a pie of which he was still more fond, capped by black coffee, all of which articles, except the last-named, were prepared by the hostess, who, in faultless toilette, with remarkably brilliant color, smilingly welcomed her husband and his guests to the half-past six dinner. When they had gone to the theatre, and the mother had talked to her two sons of the day's school experiences, before they settled down to their evening of study, she returned to the dining-room, and, as Mary had a headache and had had a busy day, she assisted in washing and wiping the unusual number of soiled dishes, and in setting the breakfast table. At nine o'clock she dragged her weary self upstairs. As she passed the door of her sanctum on the way to her bed-chamber, she paused, then entered, and lighted the gas-jet over her desk. On it lay the page of foolscap, blank but for the words:

"He was—"

The day had gone and the plot with it.

With a half-sob she sat down and wrote with tired and trembling fingers:

"He was—this morning. He isn't now!"

But will not my readers agree with me that she was a genuine wife, mother, housekeeper,—in short, a "chink-filler?"

CHAPTER VII

MUST-HAVES AND MAY-BES

"A Summer in Leslie Goldthwaite's Life," one of the most charming, as well as one of the most helpful of Adeline D.T. Whitney's books, was sent into the world over a quarter-century ago. But age cannot wither nor custom stale, nor render old-fashioned the delightful volume with its many quaint and original ideas. Others besides girls have learned the practical truth of one sentence which, for the good it has done, deserves to be written in letters of gold:

"Something must be crowded out."

More than one perplexed and conscientious worker has, like myself, written it out in large text and tacked it up in sewing-room, kitchen, or over a desk.

In the beginning, I want to guard what may seem to be a weak point by stating, first and above all, that this is not an excuse for slighting or "slurring over" our legitimate work.

One easygoing housekeeper used to say that, in her opinion, there was a genius in slighting. Her home attested the fact that she had reduced the habit of leaving things undone to a science, but it is doubtful if the so-called genius differed largely from that which forms a prominent characteristic of

Marion Harland

the porcine mother, and enables her to enjoy her home and little ones with apparent indifference to the fact that outsiders denominate one a sty, and her offspring small pigs.

Not very long ago I was frequently brought into contact with a woman who has, as all her friends acknowledge, a faculty for "turning off work." She has a jaunty knack of pinning trimming on a hat, which, although bare and stiff in the start, evolves into a toque or capote that a French milliner need not blush to confess as her handiwork. She can run up the seams in a dress-skirt with speed that fills the slower sisters working at her side with sad envy. She puts up preserves with marvelous dexterity, and can toss together eggs, butter, sugar and flour, and turn out a cake in less time than an ordinary woman would consume in creaming the butter and sugar. But it is an obvious fact that the work of this remarkable woman lacks "staying power." Her too rapid and long stitches often give way, allowing between them mortifying glimpses of white under-waist or skirt to obtrude themselves; in a high wind the trimmings or feathers are likely to blow loose from the dainty bonnets; her preserves ferment, and have to be "boiled down," while the cutting of her cake reveals the truth that under the top-crust are heavy streaks, like a stratum of igneous formation shot athwart the aqueous. The maker of gown, hat, preserves, and cake lacks thoroughness. As one irreverent young man once said after dancing with her—"she is all the time tumbling to pieces."

Since something must be crowded out, the first and great point is to determine what this something must be. Certain duties are of prime importance, others only secondary. One writer says of a woman who had cultivated the sense of proportion with regard to her work: "We felt all the while the cheer and gladness and brightness of her presence, just because she had learned to make this great distinction,—to put some things first and others second. She had mastered the great secret of life."

This talk of mine reminds me of a prosy preacher who chose one Sunday as the text of his sermon, "It is good to be here," and began his discourse with the announcement, "I shall employ all the time this morning in telling of the places in which it is *not* good to be. If you come to hear me to-night I will tell you where it is good to be."

So we will consider the things which must not be put aside. Some duties are plain, self-evident, and heaven-appointed. Such is the care of children. To the young mother this is, or should be, the first and great object in life. Her baby must have enough clothes, and these clothes must be kept clean, fresh and dainty, for his pure, sweet babyship. His many little wants must be attended to, even if calls are not returned and correspondence is neglected. But it is not absolutely necessary to load down the tiny frocks with laces and embroidery that are time consumers from the moment they are stitched on till the article they serve to adorn is ready for the rag-bag. The starching, the fluting, the ironing, all take precious hours that might be employed upon some of the must-haves.

Home duties take the precedence of social engagements. A busy mother cannot serve John, babies and society with all her heart, soul and strength. Either she will neglect the one and cleave unto the other, or neither will receive proper attention. Even a wealthy woman who can make work easy (?) by having a nurse for each child in the household, cannot afford to leave the tender oversight of the clothes, food, and general health of one of her babies to those hired to do the "nursing." There is no genuine nurse but the mother; and although others may do well under her eye and directed by her, she can never shift the mother-responsibility to other shoulders; and if she be worthy of the dignity of mother-hood, she will never wish to have it otherwise.

A few days ago I heard a clever woman say that a friend of

Marion Harland

hers had chosen as her epitaph—not, "She hath done what she could," but "She tried to do what she couldn't," and that her motto in life seemed to be, "What's worth doing at all is worth doing *swell*." This speech applies to too many American women, and so general is the habit of over-crowding, that she who would really determine what is worth doing at all must hold herself calmly and quietly in hand, and stand still with closed eyes for one minute, until her senses, dazed by the wild rush about her, have become sufficiently clear, and her hand steady enough, to pick out the diamonds of duty from the glass chips which pass with the superficial observer for first-water gems. It is well for our housewife to have some test-stone duty by which she may rate the importance of other tasks. Such a test-stone may be John's or baby's needs or requirements. Of course she must not expect to make as much show to the outside world by keeping the children well and happy, entertaining her husband each evening until he forgets the trials and vexations of his business-day, preparing toothsome and wholesome dainties for the loved ones, and making home sweet and attractive, as does the society woman who attends twenty teas a week, gives large lunches and dinners, and "takes in" every play and opera.

"The little bird sits at his door in the sun,
Atilt like a blossom among the leaves,
And lets his illumined being o'errun
With the deluge of summer it receives.
His mate feels the eggs beneath her wings,
And the heart in her dumb breast flutters and sings;
He sings to the wide world, and she to her nest;
In the nice ear of Nature which song is the best?"

If my reader is a mother it will not take very long for her to justly determine the values.

Recently I heard a busy woman and an excellent housewife

say: "If I am pressed with important work, and my parlors are not very dusty, I unblushingly wipe off the polished furniture, on which every speck shows, and leave the upholstered articles until another time."

This was not untidiness. It was only putting time and work to the best advantage, that there might be enough to go around.

I read the other day in the woman's department of a prominent paper a letter from a subscriber who said that she was so driven with work that it was all she could do to get her washing done, much less her ironing. So she had determined to use her bed-linen and underclothing rough-dry. Would it not have been wiser as well as neater, for her to have plain, untrimmed underwear, and iron it without starching? For here comfort is also to be considered. Is not smooth, neat linen to take the precedence of trimming and starch?

Another thing which must not be crowded out is rest, and the care of the health,—and the one includes the other. A day in which no breathing-space has been found is a wicked day. Not only is it our duty to the bodies which God has given to care properly for them, but it is, moreover, a positive duty to our fellow-man. An overworked person is likely to be cross and disagreeable, for the mind is affected by the state of the body, and it is an absolute sin to put ourselves into a condition that makes others miserable. It is also wretched economy to burn the candle at both ends every day. When it is needed to aid us in some large piece of work the wick will be consumed, and the light will faintly flicker, or splutter feebly and die.

Among the things which may be easily and advantageously crowded out, we may rank unnecessary talking. The house-keeper would be surprised were she to take note of the time

Marion Harland

spent by her servants, and, perhaps, even by herself, in saying a few words here, and telling a story there in the time which rightfully belongs to other tasks. Could she look, herself unseen, into her kitchen, she would find Bridget and Norah, arms akimbo, comparing notes as to past "places" or present beaux. Gossip is their meat and drink, and it does not occur to them, or they do not care, that they are paid the same wages for time thus spent as for the hours at the tubs and ironing-board. "When you work, work; and when you play, play," is an excellent motto for both mistress and maid.

To many workers there is a lack of courage and a sinking of heart at the thought of a large piece of work ahead of them, and such persons lose a vast amount of time in looking at a duty before they attack it. This habit of dallying over a task is something which may certainly be crowded out.

The two great points in the successful management of time are concentration and system. At the beginning of each day set duties in array before your mind's eye, and attack them, one at a time. This may at first sight sound like ridiculously unnecessary advice. But unless my readers are exceptional women, they all know what it is to be so pressed with things that must be done that they do not know what to begin first. Having chosen the most important task, attack that, and when you have once laid hold of the plough, drive straight ahead, not allowing the sight of another furrow, which is not just straight, to induce you to stop midway to straighten it before you have finished the one upon which your energies should now be bent. Too many women are mere potterers, not earnest laborers. They begin to make a bed, and stop to brush up some dust that has collected under the bureau. Before the dust-pan is emptied, the thought occurs of a tear in one of the children's aprons, and by the time that is mended, something else appears that needs attention, and all day long tasks are half completed and nothing is entirely finished, until at night the poor toiler is weary and discouraged, with nothing to show for her pains, except an anxious face and a semi-straight household.

Woman's work is quite as dignified as man's, and why should it not be arranged as carefully and systematically? If some thing must be crowded out, let it be, with forethought and reason, set to one side,—not shoved or huddled amid mess and confusion.

Marion Harland

CHAPTER VIII

WHAT GOOD WILL IT DO?

Thus I translate the Latin *cui bono*. In whatever language the query is put, it is the most valuable balance-wheel ever attached to human action and speech.

The principle is old. The pithy phrase in the shrewd Roman's mouth was two-edged, and had a sharp point. The enterprise that led to no good was not worth beginning.

A friend of mine who has written long, much, and, so far as I can judge, always profitably, told me that in 1865 she wrought out what was, to her apprehension, the most powerful book she ever composed,—a story of the Civil War. She was a Unionist in every thought and sentiment, and this she proclaimed; she had had unusual opportunities of seeing behind the scenes of political intrigue, and she had improved them. When the last chapter was written she carried the MS. into her husband's study at dusk one evening, and began to read it aloud to him. She finished it at two o'clock a.m. Her auditor would not let her pause until then. Hoarse, but with a heart beating high with excitement, she waited for the verdict. The husband walked up and down the floor for some minutes, head bent and hands clasped behind him, deep in thought. Finally he stopped in front of her.

"That is a marvelous book, my dear,—strong, true, dramatic. It will sell well. It will make a noise in the world. But—*cui bono?*"

Chagrined, mortified, angry, the author took the words with her to her room, and her brain tossed upon them as upon thorns all night. At dawn she arose and put the MS. into the fire.

"I shudder to this day in thinking what would have been had I acted differently," she says. "What I had written in a semi-frenzy of patriotism would have been hot pincers, tearing open wounds which humanity and religion would have taught me to heal."

Into many lives comes some such crisis, when the text I would bind upon my reader's mind would act as a break-water, and save more than one soul from sorrow, perhaps from destruction. In the everyday life of everybody, crises of less moment accentuate experience, and tend to make the nature richer or poorer.

I incline to the belief that nine-tenths of the remorseful heartaches which most of us know only too well, might be spared us did we pause to repeat to ourselves the Latin or English sentence. It may be a relic of barbarism, but it is an undeniable trait of human nature that all of us feel the longing to "answer back," or, as the children put it, to "get even with" the man or woman whose speech offends us. The apostle showed marvelous knowledge of the weakness of sinful mortals when he affirmed that the tongue was an unruly member, for it is easier to perform a herculean feat, to strain physical strength and muscle to the utmost, than to bite back the sharp retort, or repress the acrid reply. And there is such a hopelessness in the sentence once uttered! It is gone from us forever. We may regret it and show our repentance in speech and action, but we cannot blot the memory of the cruel words from our minds, or from the mind of the person,—perhaps a mere acquaintance, oftener bone of our bone and flesh of our flesh,—in whose heart the barbed arrows of our eloquence rankle for months and years. The dear friend may forgive freely and fully the bitter censure or unjust reproof, but a scar is left which, if touched in a moment of inadvertence, will pulse and throb with the remembrance of pain.

"Leave the bitter word unspoken;
So shalt thou be strongly glad,
If there lies no backward shadow
On dead faces, wan and sad."

"To repress a harsh answer, to confess a fault, to stop, right or wrong, in the midst of self-defence, in gentle submission, sometimes requires a struggle like life and death, but these three efforts are the golden threads with which domestic happiness is woven."

How frequently we exclaim,—"If I ever get the opportunity, I will give that woman a piece of my mind!" or, "I shall some time have the satisfaction of telling that man what I think of his behavior."

It is a very melancholy and most *un*satisfactory satisfaction to know that you have made a person uncomfortable. It is folly for you to suppose for a moment that an angry speech of yours will turn a man from a course of which you do not approve. It will make him hate you, perhaps, but it will not change him. It is not only foolish, but un-Christian to triumph in another's discomfiture. Then why "give the piece of your mind," which you can never take back? What good will it do?

The same question may be asked with regard to the uncharitable remarks which nearly all of us make daily.

Once in a great while, we meet a human being, still permitted to dwell on this sinful earth, who rarely says anything unkind of anybody, whose rule is, "If you cannot say a kind thing say nothing." In the course of a long and varied experience I may have known half-a-dozen such. But what man has done, man may do again. What is the baneful spirit which tempts the gentlest of us to take more pleasure in calling attention to a fault than to a virtue? If a woman is a tender mother, a model wife, and an excellent house-keeper, why, when her virtues are discussed, is it necessary for some one to "think it is such a pity that she does not read more?" or what good comes from the remark that she is "sprightly, but not very deep?"

There is no habit more easily contracted than that of wholesale criticism, and it is a habit that grows with fungus-like rapidity. Washington Irving says "that a sharp tongue is the only edged tool that grows keener with constant use," and with many people the unruly member has acquired a razor-like edge which contains in itself the faculty of keeping sharp, and never needs "honing" or "setting."

I have in mind one man to whom I hesitate to name a friend, unless it chances to be one over whom he has cast the mantle of his approval. Those who are fortunate enough to live up to his standard are very few, and all others he criticises unmercifully, employing in his condemnation a ready wit and fluent speech that might be used in a nobler purpose. Such a reputation as he holds for all unchari-tableness is not an enviable one, and one wonders what would be his answer to our *cui bono*. When there are so many truthful and pleasant things that may be said of everybody, why call attention to disagreeable points, which after all, are fewer than the agreeable ones?

The office of the gossip is so thankless that it is a marvel any one accepts it. To certain natures there is positive delight in being the first to relate a choice bit of scandal. It never occurs to them that the old maxim with regard to a dog who fetches a bone can possibly be applied to them. But it is as true as the stars that if a person brings you an unsavory tale of a friend, she will carry away as ugly a story of you, if she can find the faintest suggestion upon which to found it. The gossip acquires a detective-like faculty for following out a clue, but unfortunately, the clue is oftener purely imaginary than real. A little discrepancy like this does not disturb the professional scandal-monger. So tenacious is the habit of making much of nothing, that, deprived of this, her sustenance, she would find life colorless and void. So, if material does not present itself, she manufactures it. One must live.

There is also a habit, which, while comparatively innocent, is likely to bring trouble upon the perpetrator. It is that of making many confidantes. Here comes a very serious *cui bono*. Undoubtedly there is a momentary satisfaction in telling one's woes and sorrows to an interested listener. When the auditor is a friend, and a trusted friend, whose sympathy is genuine and whose discretion is vast, there is a comfort beyond description in unburdening one's soul. But there is a line to be drawn even here. It is not deceit to keep your private affairs to yourself when you are sure that you are guilty of nothing dishonorable or hypocritical in so doing. You are often your own best and safest counselor. I know one woman who long ago said a thing which should be a motto to those susceptible persons who in a sudden expansion of the heart tell all they know and which they would most wish to keep to themselves.

"My dear," she said, "in the course of a somewhat checkered life I have discovered that while I have often been sorry for things which I have told, I have never had cause to regret what I have kept to myself."

If you have a secret and wish to keep it, guard it jealously. It ceases to be yours alone when you impart it to another. Your confidante may be discretion personified, and, yet again, she may have some nearer and dearer one to whom she "tells everything," even the secrets of her friends. Or, you may in time learn to be ashamed of the confidence which you have reposed in this person, and the knowledge that she knows and remembers the thing, and, it may be, knows that you feel a mortification at the thought of it, will gall you unspeakably.

Perhaps the hardest struggle that comes to the average human being is to let others be mistaken. Yet what good will it do to point out to them their mistakes? If your husband or son tells several people that he met John Smith last week in New York, and you know that he was in that city three weeks ago, why correct him? He is talking hastily and does not stop to measure his words or time. The mistake is unimportant. Why antagonize a man by exclaiming:

"My dear John! This is the third week in January, and you went to New York immediately after Christmas."

When you hear your friend tell your favorite story, and change some minor detail, she will love you not a whit the more if you correct her with—

"No, Mary! the way it happened was this"—and then proceed with the tale in the manner which you consider best.

There are so many things which we all do for which there is no honest reason, that I will mention only one more. That is the exceedingly uncomfortable trick of reminding a man of something he has once said, when he has since had occasion to change his mind. Perhaps some years ago when you first met your now dear friend, you thought her manner affected, and did not hesitate to mention the fact to your family. Since then you have become so well acquainted with her delightful points that you forget your early impression of her. How do you feel when you are enthusiastically enumerating her many lovable attributes, if the member of the household with the fiendish memory strikes in with—

"Oh, then you have changed your mind about her? You remember you once said that you considered her the most affected mortal whom you had ever met."

Under such provocation does not murder assume the guise of justifiable homicide?

There is no more bitter diet than to be forced to eat one's own words. Never tell one of an opinion which he once held, if he has since had reason to alter his views. There is no sin or weakness in changing one's mind. It is a thing which all of us—if we except a few victims to pig-headed prejudice—do daily. And, as a rule, we hate to be reminded of the fact. Then why call the attention of others to the circumstances that they are guilty of the same weakness, if such it be? Again I ask, *cui bono?*

CHAPTER IX

SHALL, I PASS IT ON?

"Me refrunce, mum!"

I look up, bewildered, from an essay to which I have just set the caption—"Who is my Neighbor?"

"Me carackter, mum! Me stiffticket! You'll not be sending me away without one, peticklerly as 'twas meself as give warnin'?"

She is ready for departure. Dressed in decent black for the brother "who was drownded las' summer," she stands at the back of my desk, one hand on her hip, and makes her demand. It is not a petition, but a dispassionate statement of a case that has no other side.

She has been in my kitchen for six months as my nominal servitor. She has drawn her wages punctually for that time. She "wants a change;" her month is up; she is going out of my house, out of my employ, out of my life. These things being true, Katy wants to take with her all that pertains to her. One of these belongings is her "refrunce." From her standpoint, I owe it to her as truly as I owed the sixteen dollars I have just paid her.

I engaged Katy last May from a highly responsible intelligence office. For and in consideration of a fee of three dollars, a lady-like agent, with a smooth voice and demeanor, passed over "the girl" to me as she might a brown paper parcel of moist sugar. She supplied, gratis, a personal voucher for the woman I had engaged, having known her well for five years. Katy had, moreover, a model "recommend," which she unwrapped from a bit of newspaper that had kept it clean. The chirography was the fashionable "long English;" the diction was good, and the orthography faultless. Envelope and paper had evidently come from a lady's davenport.

"This is to certify that Katherine Brady has lived in my family for eleven months as cook. I have found her industrious, sober, neat, honest and obliging. She also understands her business thoroughly. She leaves me in consequence of my removal from the city. (Mrs.) ... No ... West 57th St., New York City."

If the certificate had a fault, it was that the fit was too nearly perfect. I had heard of references written to order by venal scribes, and I consulted the city directory. Mr. ...'s office was in Wall street, his residence No ... West 57th street. I called to see him, found him in, and found him a gentleman. He had no doubt that all was right. He believed the name of their latest cook was Katherine. They called her "Katy." He knew that his wife was sorry to part with her, and inferred that she was a worthy woman.

We, too, were leaving town, but only for the summer. Katy "liked the country in hot weather. All the best fam'lies now-a-days had their country-places."

It is not an easy matter to "change help" during a summer sojourn in a cottage distant an hour and a half from town. The act involves one or more railway journeys, much running about in hot streets, and much hopeless ringing at dumb and dusty doors. This is the explanation of Katy's six months' stay in my kitchen. In town, she would have been dismissed at the end of the first week. She was a wretched cook, and a worse laundress. Within an hour after she entered my door, the decent black gown was exchanged for a dingy calico which she wore, without a collar, and minus a majority of the buttons, all day long and every day. She was "a settled girl"—owning to twenty-eight summers, and having weathered forty winters. Her hair, streaked with gray, tumbled down as persistently as Patience Riderhood's, and was uncomfortably easy of identification in *ragout* and muffins. Her slippers were down at heel; her kitchen was never in order; her tins were black; her pots were greasy; her range was dull; her floors unclean. Like all her compeers, she "found the place harder nor she had been give to onderstand, but was willin' to do her best, seein' she had come."

Her best was sometimes sour bread, sometimes burned biscuits, generally weak, muddy coffee, always under-seasoned vegetables and over-seasoned soup. By July 1, she developed a genius for quarreling with the other servants that got up a domestic hurricane, and I told her she must leave. She promptly burst into tears, and reminded me that I "had engaged her for the sayson, an' what would a pore girl be doin' in the empty city in the middle of the summer?

"An' whativer they may say o' me ways down-stairs, it's the timper of a babby I have, an' would niver throw a harrd wurrd at a dog, let alone a human. Whin they think me cross, it's only that I'm a bit quoiet, an' who can wonder? thinkin' o' me pore brother as was drownded las' summer, an' him niver out o' me moind!"

I weakly allowed her to stay upon promise of good and peaceable behavior, and tried to make the best of her, as she had of the place.

One September day, just when the physician, called in to see a dear young guest, had expressed his fear that she was sickening for a serious illness, Katy gave warning. "Her feelin's would not allow her to stay in a house where there was sickness. It always reminded her of her pore, dear brother what was drownded las' summer, an' a sick pairson made a quare lot o' extra work, even when it was considered in the wages. She'd be lavin' that day week, her month bein' up then."

Happily, the threatening of illness was a false alarm, but Katy is going. The city is filling up, and many "best families" must re-open their town-houses in time for the school terms. She looks as happy at the prospect of a return to area-gossip and Sunday flirtation as I feel at getting rid of her. I have made with her a farewell round of pantries, refrigerator, and cellar. Valuable articles are missing—notably two solid silver tablespoons and a dozen fine napkins. At the back of the barn a pile of brushwood masks a Monte Testaccio of china and cut-glass. Dirt is in every corner; glass-towels have been degraded into dish and floor-cloths; saucepans are burned into holes; tops are lacking to pots and pails.

For all this there is no redress. When I made a stand upon the "case of spoons," as being old family silver, the house-maid declared that Katy had used them often to stir soup and porridge, and Katy retorted with gusts of brine and brogue that she "wouldn't be accountable for things that didn't belong to her business."

Altogether, my amiable willingness that she should take her leave without shaking more dust from her feet upon an already burdened household, had become impatient desire by the time I counted out her wages. Yet, here she stands, grim as the sphinx, fixed as Fate, with the inexorable requisition, "Me refrunce, mum!"

"What could I say of you Katy?" I ask, miserably.

"What any leddy whatsomever, as *is* a leddy, would say! What lots o' other leddies, as leddylike as enny leddy could wish to be, ridin' in their coaches an' livin' in houses tin times 's big as this, leddies as had none but leddylike ways, has said!" is the tautological response. "I've served yez, fair an' faithful, for six mont's, and it stan's to rayson as I wouldn't 'a' been let to stay that long onder yer ruff if so be I hadn't shuited yez."

She has me there, and she knows it. Inwardly, I retract some of the hard things I have thought and said of Mrs. ... of No ... West Fifty-seventh street. Having let the creature abide under her roof for eleven months, she must justify herself for the act. She meant to leave town, as I mean to go back to town, and, like me, truckled weakly to expediency. Nevertheless, her weakness did me a real wrong.

Shall I pass it on?

This is the moral question I would sift from what my readers may regard as trivial and commonplace details. The fact that my experience is so common as to seem trite, is the most startling feature in the case. Our American domestic service is a loosely woven web, full of snarls and knots. It is time that the great national principle that government must depend upon the consent of the governed, should be studied and applied to the matter in hand. We, the wage-payers, are the governed, and without our consent. The recent attempt to enforce this retroverted law upon a grand scale, in calling a mighty railway corporation to account for the discharge of a dozen or so out of several thousand employes, is no stronger proof of this curious reversal of positions than the demand of my whilom cook that I should set my hand to a lie.

I caught her once in a falsehood so flagrant that I commended the rule of truth-speaking to her moral sense, and asked how she reconciled the sin with her knowledge of what was right.

Her answer was ready: "Oh, there's no sin in a lie that doesn't hurt yer neighbor!"

Judged even by this easygoing principle, I should sin in penning the reference without which Katy intimates that she will not withdraw her foot from my house. She looms before me,—vulgar, determined, irrational and ignorant,— the impersonation of the System under which we cringe and groan.

"What would you do?" I ask a friend, who is a successful housewife.

She shrugs her shoulders.

"Oh, swim with the tide! Not to give the certificate will be equivalent to boycotting yourself. The news of your contumacy will spread like prairie fires. You will be baited and banned beyond endurance."

"But—my duty to my neighbor?"

"Thanks to the prevailing rule in these affairs, your neighbor knows how little a written reference is worth. She will satisfy the proprieties by reading it, and form her own opinion of the girl. When Katy has worn out her saucepans and patience, your successor in misfortune will give her clean papers to the next place. It is a sort of endless chain of suffering. Then, there is the humane side of the question. A recommendation of some sort is a form most housewives insist upon. You may be taking the bread out of a 'girl's' mouth by denying her a scrap of paper."

Nevertheless, I shall not give Katy a reference. I have said to her in plain but temperate terms:

"You are a poor cook. You are wasteful, dirty, ill-tempered and impertinent. You have been a grievous trial and a money loss to me. I am willing to write this down, together with the statement that you are sober, strong and quick to learn, and that you would probably work well under a stricter mistress than I have time to be."

She has informed me in *in*temperate terms, that "it is aisy to see you are no leddy, an' fer the matter o' that, no Christian, ayther, or you'd not put sech an insult on to an honest, harrd-wurkin' girrl as has her livin' to git."

She pronounces furthermore, that she "was niver so put upon an' put about in all her life afore as since into this house she come;" that she "will have the law o' me for refusing her her rights." Finally, and most intemperately, that "the Lord will dale with me for grindin' the face of a pore, defenceless young cre'tur' as has had such a pile o' throuble already. If her pore, dear brother what was drownded las' summer was alive, I wouldn't dare trate her so cruel."

I stand fast, between breaths, to my resolution. I relate the true history of the transaction to enforce my appeal to my fellow housekeepers, all over the land, to join hands in a measure which would, I am persuaded, go far toward rectifying a crooked system.

Let each housekeeper, in dismissing a servant, write out without prejudice for or against the late employee, her claims to the confidence of the next employer, and her faults,—in short, a veritable "character." Let her pledge herself to her sister-housekeepers and to her conscience, not to receive into her family one who cannot produce satisfactory testimonials of her fitness for the place she seeks.

In England, a mistress who engages a maid without such credentials is regarded as recreant to her order. In England, too, the former mistress is held partly responsible for the mischief done, if she turn loose upon other households a woman like Katherine Brady.

The proposed remedy for a crying and a growing evil is so simple that some may doubt its practical efficacy. Yet the most casual thinker must see the strength as well as the simplicity of a plan which would make skill and fidelity in service the only road to success. Self-interest, if nothing else, would stimulate our Katies and Bridgets, our Dinahs and our Gretchens, to keep a place, if it were not so wickedly easy to "make a change." Our kitchens are overrun and ravaged by Arabs that become, every year, more despotic.

"Who would be free, herself must strike the blow." General liberty from this bondage can only be achieved by determined and united effort. The establishment in every community of a simple organization under the name of The Housekeepers' Protective Union, that should have but one article in its constitution, and that one be the pledge I have indicated, would cover the whole ground, and effect within a year, permanent reform. Shall not this appeal be the Alexander to cut the Gordian knot which has, thus far, defied the dexterity and strength of all who have wrestled with the problem?

Who will send me news of the formation of the first Chapter of the H.P.U.?

CHAPTER X

"ONLY HER NERVES."

There is a slang expression current among the irreverent youth of the present day, when referring to a man wise in his own conceit, to the effect that "what that fellow does not know is torn out." So I, quoting my juniors, begin my talk with the sentence—for the raciness of which I apologize— "What American women do not know about nervousness is torn out!"

Only this week in a city horse-car I watched the faces of my fellow-passengers,—women, most of them—with a pain at my heart. Oh, the tired, strained, impatient faces, and the eager, alert, and anxious expression that belong to the people of this new and free country! Some of these wretched mortals had babies with them,—babies whose fretful wails seemed but to voice the mother's expression of countenance. In an uneasy way the little mites would be shifted from one shoulder to another, or trotted in nervousness that reminded me irresistibly of the nursery rhyme which might be the motto of the American mother:

> ", out of breath,
> They trot the baby, most to death,
> Sick or well, or cold or hot,
> It's trottery, trottery, trottery, trot."

Marion Harland

Of all these women there was not one who sat still for three consecutive minutes. Heads were twisted to look at the name of the corner lamp-posts, glove fingers were smoothed, the folds of dress-skirts shaken out, hats straightened,—until I would fain have cried out in irreverent paraphrase, at sight of the unrest which I blush to confess made me conscious of my own nerves:

"Not one sitteth still—no, not one!"

That men have any patience with what they term "feminine fidgetiness," is but an evidence that they are better Christians than we of the gentler sex are willing to admit. For I think I am not making a sweeping assertion when I state that not one tolerably healthy man in five hundred knows what it is to have nerves such as are the birthright of his mother, sister, and wife. And yet how well the physician, poet, autocrat and professor, Oliver Wendell Holmes, knows and sympathizes with this weakness in us! He touches the truth in a direct way that wrings a sigh of familiar pain from many a patient soul.

"Some people have a scale of your whole nervous system and can play all the gamut of your sensibilities in semi-tones, touching the naked nerve-pulps as a pianist strikes the keys of his instrument. I am satisfied that there are as great masters of this nerve-playing as Vieuxtemps or Thalberg in their lines of performance. Married life is the school in which the most accomplished artists in this department are found. A delicate woman is the best instrument; she has such a magnificent compass of sensibilities. From the deep inward moan which follows pressure on the great nerves of right, to the sharp cry as the filaments of taste are struck with a crashing sweep, is a range which no other instrument possesses."

And again he speaks of the less serious affection of the

nerves as: ... "Not fear, but what I call nervousness,—unreasoning, but irresistible; as when, for instance, one, looking at the sun going down, says: 'I will count fifty before it disappears,' and as he goes on and it becomes doubtful whether he will reach the number, he gets strangely flurried, and his imagination pictures life and death and heaven and hell as the issues depending on the completion or non-completion of the fifty he is counting."

If a man can describe it all so well, what could a woman do? I fear that her description would be too graphic to be read by us, her sisters.

Many people have a way of saying of a sufferer:

"There is nothing the matter with her. She is only excessively nervous."

This "only" is a very serious matter. There is no illness more difficult to treat and more trying to bear than nervous prostration. It is a slowly advancing malady which is scarcely recognized as serious by one's friends until the tired mind succumbs and mental aberration is the terrible finale of the seemingly slight indisposition.

My readers may wonder why I dwell upon a subject that baffles even the most eminent physicians in the country. It is because I feel that each of us women has in herself the only check to the nervousness which we all dread. We, as Americans, cannot afford to trifle with our unfortunate inheritance, but must use every means at our command to subjugate the evil instead of being subjugated by it. Too many women, especially among the lower classes, think it "pretty" to be nervous. The country practitioner will tell you of the precious hours he loses every week in hearkening to the recital of personal discomforts as poured into his professional ears by farmers' wives. And the beginning,

Marion Harland

middle, and end of all their plaints is "my nerves." Anything, from a sprained ankle to consumption, is attributed to or augmented by these necessary adjuncts to the human anatomy.

Not long ago I was talking to the ignorant mother of a jaundiced, colicky child of two years of age.

"What does she eat?" I asked.

"Well, she takes fancies, and her latest notion is that she won't eat nothin' but ginger-nuts and bananas. So she mostly lives on them. Sometimes she suffers awful."

"From indigestion?"

"Oh, no!" patronizingly. "She inherits all my nervous weakness. Her nerves get the upper hand of her, and she turns pale and shivers all over, and then she looks as if she would go into the spasms."

"But," I suggested, "don't you think that is caused by acute indigestion?"

"No, ma'am. You see I know what it is, havin' had it so bad myself. The nerves of her stomach all draw up, and cause the shakin' and tremblin'."

Suggestions as to the modification of the little one's diet were useless. Indigestion was unromantic (in the mother's judgment), and "nerves" were highly aristocratic and refined.

I am happy to note that the girl of the rising generation is learning that to succumb to weakness is not a sign of ladyhood. She does not jump on a chair at sight of a mouse, scream when she meets a cow in a country road, or cover her face and shudder at mention of a snake. She is proud of being afraid of nothing, of having a good appetite, and of the ability to sleep as soundly as a tired and healthy child.

It is not then to her, but to ourselves, that we mothers have need to look. We are too often the ones who give way to hysterical tears or to sharp words, or perhaps to unjust criticism, all of which we attribute to nervousness. Our more frank girl, if affected in the same way, would bluntly acknowledge that she was "as cross as a bear." Let us quietly take hold of ourselves and ask ourselves the plain question, "Are we nervous, or cross?" If the latter, we know how to remedy it. A well person has no right to be so abominably bad-tempered or moody that he cannot keep people from finding it out. If you are nervous, there is some reason for it. Perhaps you did not sleep well last night; perhaps you are suffering from dyspepsia; but in any case will-power will do much towards lessening the trouble. If you are ill, it may cause a struggle greater than your nearest and dearest can imagine to repress the startled ejaculation at the slamming of a door, or the angry exclamation when your bed is jarred. But you will be better, not worse, physically, for this self-control. The woman, who, though tortured by nervousness sets her teeth and says, "I *will* be strong!" stands a better chance of speedy recovery than does she who weakly gives way to hysterical sobs a dozen times a day. Your nerves should be your servants, and, like all servants, may give you much trouble, but as long as you are mistress of yourself you need not fear them. Once let them get the control over you, and you are gone. There is no tyrant more merciless than he who has hitherto been a slave.

May I add one word to those whom we, in exasperation, are apt to call aggressively strong? If you, yourself, do not know what nervousness is, pity and help the poor sufferer in your family who never knows during day or night what it is to be without what you consider "the fussiness that sets you wild."

If this mother, or aunt, or sister, does control herself, remember that she is stronger than you, as the man who successfully curbs the fiery steed is more to be commended for courage than he who holds the reins loosely over the back of the safe farm-horse who does not know how to shy, kick, or run.

CHAPTER XI

THE RULE OF TWO

One character mentioned in the unique rhyme of Mary and her Little Lamb, has never had due praise and consideration dealt out to him. The teacher who heartlessly expelled from the temple of learning the unoffending and guileless companion of the innocent maiden who is the heroine of the above-mentioned ditty, was, in spite of his cruelty, a philosopher. After the exit of the principal actors in the poem, we are told that the following conversation ensued:

> "What makes the lamb love Mary so?"
> The eager children cry.
> "Because she loves the lamb, you know,"
> The teacher did reply.

The teacher was wise in his generation. In his "reply," lies a world of meaning—one of the answers to the old question of the reason for personal antipathies and attractions, and may perhaps be said, in this case, to touch upon animal magnetism.

There are exceptions to every rule, and to the maxim that "love begets love" there are many instances to be cited in which the contrary proves true. We all have been so unfortunate at some time during our lives as to be liked by

Marion Harland

people of whom we were not fond. But, if we look the matter thoughtfully and honestly in the face, we will acknowledge that in ninety-nine cases out of a hundred we are attracted toward a person as soon as we learn that that person finds us agreeable. Of course this knowledge must not be conveyed in a manner that disgusts by effusiveness a sensitive person. None of us like fulsome flattery, but a compliment so delicately hinted that it does not shock, and scarcely surprises the person for whom it is intended, seldom fails to produce an impression that is far from disagreeable. Certainly no more graceful compliment can be paid a man or woman by us selfish mortals than the acknowledgment of an affinity between ourselves and the person whom we would honor by our friendship. Said a well-known scholar to me:

"The most laudatory public speech ever addressed to me failed to make my heart glow as warmly as did the remark of an old friend not long ago. We had been separated for years, and at our reunion spent the first hour in talking of old times, etc. Suddenly, my friend turned to me, and grasping my hand exclaimed:

"Old fellow! you always were, and still are, my affinity!"

"The subtle flattery of that one exclamation makes me even now thrill with a delicious throb of self-conceit."

Not long ago, I asked of an acquaintance who is a wonderful reader of character:

"Why has Mrs. S—so many good friends?"

"Because she is such a good friend herself."

"But why is she attractive to so many people?" queried I.

"Because she is first attracted by them," was the quick response. "She goes on the principle that there is some good in everybody, and sets herself to work to find it. Each of us knows when she is thrown into contact with a person who likes her. It is as if each were surrounded with tinted atmospheres,—some green, some blue, some red, or yellow—in fact, there are more shades and colors than you can mention. When two reds meet, they mingle; when two harmonious tints touch, they may form a pleasing combination; but when such enemies as blue and green come together, they clash—fairly 'swear at one another,' and the persons enveloped in the opposing atmospheres are mutually disagreeable. The man who is surrounded by the color capable of most harmonious combinations is said to have personal magnetism."

May not this explanation, while rather far-fetched, afford some clue to the causes of personal popularity? And the thought following swift upon this is: If this be true, how much may each of us have to do with softening and making capable of harmony his and her own individual atmosphere? While we cannot change our "colors" (to follow out my friend's figure) we may shade them down and make them less pronounced, so that in time they may become capable of a variety of combinations.

Does not Faber touch upon this point, when he says:

> "The discord is within which jars
> So roughly in life's song;
> 'Tis we ourselves who are at fault
> When others seem so wrong,"

We blame others for being uncongenial When the "discord is within," that makes all things go awry. A drunken man sees the whole world go around, and blames it, for its unsteadiness.

One way to render less obtrusive an inharmonious color, if we possess such is to keep it out of a strong light that will attract all eyes to it. Do not let us be proud of our personal defects and peculiarities. They are subjects for regret, not pride. When a woman boasts that she "knows she is often impatient, but she simply cannot help it, she is so peculiarly constituted!" she acknowledges a weakness of which she should be ashamed. If she is so undisciplined, so untrained, that she cannot avoid making life uncomfortable for those around her, she would better stay in a room by herself until she learns self-control. Often the very eccentricities of character to which we cling so tenaciously are but forms of vanity. Why should our preferences, our likes or dislikes be of more account than those of thousands of other people?

Another great mistake we make is that we try the effect of other colors with our own, and resent it hotly if they do not "go well together." We do not insist that they shall be like ours in tint, but they must act as good backgrounds, or form pleasing combinations with ours, or we will none of them. Now it is quite possible for human beings to hold contrary views from those entertained by you and me, and still be excellent members of society and reputable Christians. To many of us this seems incredible, but it is none the less true. Not only are individual characters different, but environment and education make us what we are. Very often a person who is uncongenial to us, will, in the surroundings to which she is fitted, be at ease, and perhaps even attractive.

I do not say that we must like everybody. That is a physical, mental and moral impossibility. But we may do others the justice of seeing their good traits as well as the bad. And sometimes when we find a chance acquaintance drearily uninteresting, it is because we do not take the trouble to find out what is in her.

Some people are always bored. May it not be because they

look at everything animate and inanimate from a selfish standpoint, with the query in their minds, "How does that affect me?" The old definition of a bore as "a person who talks so much of himself that he gives you no chance to talk of yourself," may apply not only to the bore, but to the bored. When you find yourself wearied and uninterested, be honest enough to examine yourself calmly, and see if the reason is not because your *vis-a-vis* is not talking about anything which interests you especially. Should he turn the conversation upon your favorite occupation or pastime, or even upon your personal likes and dislikes (which, by the way, might be an infinite bore to him), would he not at once become entertaining?

Viewed from a selfish and politic standpoint, it is to our interest to make the best of everybody. We cannot always pick and choose our associates in the school of life, and must frequently be thrown with people whom we do not "take to," and, worse still, who may not "take to" us. Since this be true, would it not be better for us to look at their pleasantest side, and, by making ourselves agreeable to them, insure their friendly feeling for us? The old saying that the good-will of a dog is preferable to his ill-will, may still be quoted with regard to many specimens of the *genus homo* which we daily meet.

There is one case in which I make an exception to all that I have said—namely, when from the first, there is—not a feeling of dislike, but a strong, uncontrollable personal antipathy. If you are generally charitable and just, and have few actual dislikes, and meet a man against whom your whole nature revolts, who is as repulsive to you as a snake would be, avoid him. It is not necessary for you to tell others of the uncomfortable impression he has made upon you. He may not affect them in the same way. I acknowledge, not only from observation, but from personal experience, that there are certain people from whom one recoils with a feeling of physical as well as mental repugnance. I believe that every woman who reads this talk has an unerring feminine instinct which will thus prompt her when she meets her own particular "Dr. Fell."

But I also believe that we seldom meet characters which repel us in this especial way. Oftener some slight to ourselves, some one unfortunate speech, biases our judgment, and those against whom we are thus prejudiced are even sometimes connected to us by ties of consanguinity. We would do well to analyze the causes which lead to our feelings of dislike, and I fear we should often find that wounded self-esteem was the root of the evil. And, after all, what a great matter a little fire kindleth! Let us quench the spark before it ignites. It is arrant folly, not to mention wickedness, to make enemies for the little while we are here. There is an incurable heartache which comes from such mistakes. Owen Meredith describes it in a poem, every verse of which throbs with hopeless love and regret, and one of which teaches a lesson so much needed by us all that we would do well to commit to memory the last two lines, and repeat them almost hourly:

> "I thought of our little quarrels and strife,
> And the letter that brought me back my ring;
> *And it all seemed then, in the waste of life,*
> *Such a very little thing!*"

CHAPTER XII

THE PERFECT WORK OF PATIENCE

A slender little treble was singing it over and over again in childish sort, with so little appreciation of the meaning of the words that the oddity of the ditty was the first thing to attract my attention to it.

> "You'd better bide a wee, wee, wee!
> Oh, you'd better bide a wee.
> La, la, la, la, la, *la*,
> You'd better bide a wee."

The elf was singing her dolly to sleep, swinging back and forth in her little rocking-chair, the waxen face pressed against the warm pink cushion of her own cheek, the yellow silk of curls palpitating with the owner's vitality mingling with the lifeless floss of her darling's wig. The picture was none the less charming because so common, but it was not in admiring contemplation of it that I arrested my pen in the middle of a word, holding it thus an inch or two above the paper in position to resume the rapid rush along the sheet it had kept up for ten minutes and more. I mused a moment. Then, with the involuntary shake one gives his cranium when he has a ringing in his ears, I finished the sentence:—"sideration, I cannot but think that patience has had her perfect work."

Marion Harland

"You'd better bide a wee!"

lisped the baby's song.

I smiled slightly and sourly at what I called mentally "the pat incongruity" of the admonition with mood and written words. A swift review of the situation confirmed the belief that I did well to be angry with the correspondent whose open letter lay upon the table beside the unfinished reply. The letter head was familiar. Of late the frequent sight of it had bred annoyance waxing into irritation. The brisk interchange of epistles grew out of a business-matter in which, as I maintained, I had been first ungenerously, then unfairly, finally dishonestly dealt with. There was no doubt in my mind of the intention to mislead, if not to defraud me, and the communication now under advisement was in tone cavalier almost to the point of insult. Aroused out of the enforced calm I had hitherto managed to preserve, I had seated myself and set my pen about the work of letting him who had now assumed the position of "that man," know how his conduct appeared in the light of reason and common sense. I had not even withheld an illusion to honesty and commercial morality. I had never done a better piece of literary work than that letter. Warming to the task in recounting the several steps of the transaction, I had not scrupled to set off my moderation by a Rembrandtish wash of shadow furnished by my correspondent's double-dealing, and to cast my civility into relief by adroit quotations from his impertinent pages. When I said that patience had had her perfect work, it was my intention to unfold in short, stinging sentences my plans as to future dealings with the delinquent.

The singing on the other side of the room meant no more than the chirping of a grasshopper upon a mullein-stalk. I did not delude myself with the notion of providential use of the tongue that tripped at the consonants and lingered in liquid dalliance with favorite vowels. Yet, after ten motion-less minutes of severe thinking, the letter was deliberately torn into strips and these into dice, and all of these went into the waste-paper basket at my elbow. I had concluded to "abide a wee." If the sun went down that once upon my anger, he arose upon cold brands and gray ashes. I had not changed my intellectual belief as to my correspondent's behavior, but the impropriety of complicating an awkward business by placing myself in the wrong to the extent of losing my temper was so obvious that I blushed in recalling the bombastic periods of the torn composition.

Since that lesson, I have never sent off an angry or splenetic letter, although the temptation to "have it out" upon paper has sometimes got the better of my more sensible self. If the excitement is particularly great, and the epistle more than usually eloquent of the fact that, as the old-time exhorters used to say, I had "great liberty of speech," I have always left it to cool over night. The "sunset dews" our mothers sang of took the starch out of the bristling pages, and the "cool, soft evening-hours," and nightly utterance of—"As we forgive them that trespass against us,"—drew out the fire.

"You'd better bide a wee!"

I have sometimes thought of writing it down, as poor Jo of "Bleak House" begged to have his last message to Esther Summerson transcribed—"werry large,"—and pasting it upon the mirror that, day by day, reflects a soberer face than I like to see in its sincere depths—as one hot and hasty soul placarded upon her looking-glass the single word "PATI-ENCE." To people whose tempers are quick and whose actions too often match their tempers, one of the most difficult of daily duties is to reserve judgment upon that which appears ambiguous in the conduct of their associates. The dreary list of slain friendships that makes retrospect painful to those of mature years; the disappointments that

Marion Harland

to the young have the bitterness of death; the tale of trusts betrayed and promises broken—how would the story be shortened and brightened if conscientious and impartial trial of the accused preceded sentence and punishment!—if, in short, we would only "bide a wee" before assuming that our friend is false, or our love unworthily given.

In a court of justice previous character counts for much. The number and respectability of the witnesses to a prisoner's excellent reputation and good behavior have almost as much weight with the jury as direct testimony in support of the claim that he did not commit the crime. To prove that he could not, without change of disposition and habit, violate the laws of his country, is the next best thing to an established alibi. I should be almost ashamed to set down a thing which everybody knows so well were it not that each one of us, when his best friend's fidelity to him is questioned, flies shamelessly in the face of reason and precedent by ignoring the record of years. He may have given ten thousand proofs of attachment to him whom he is now accused of wronging; have showed himself in a thousand ways to be absolutely incapable of deception or dishonorable behavior of any sort. A single equivocal circumstance, a word half-heard, a gesture misunderstood; the report to his prejudice of a tale-bearer who is his inferior in every respect,—any one of these outbalances the plea of memory, the appeal of reason, the consciousness of the right of the arraigned to be heard. Were not the story one of to-day and of every day, the moral turpitude it displays would arouse the hearer to generous indignation.

Taking at random one of the multitude of illustrations crowding upon my mind, let me sketch a vexatious incident of personal history. Some years ago—no matter how many, nor how long was my sojourn in the town which was the scene of the story—I accepted the invitation of an acquaintance to take a seat in her carriage while on my way to call upon a woman well known to us both. The owner of the equipage, Mrs. D—, overtook me while I was trudging up the long street leading to the suburb in which our common acquaintance lived. The day was bleak and windy, and I was glad to be spared the walk. Mrs. C—, to whom the visit was paid, came down to receive us with her hat and cloak on. She was going down town presently, she said, and would not keep us waiting while she laid aside her wraps. No! she would not have us shorten our call on her account; she could go half an hour later as well as now. A good deal was said of the disagreeable weather, and the bad sidewalks in that new section of the city—as I recollected afterward. At the time, I was more interested in her mention that her favorite brother, an editor of note from another town and State, was visiting her. She asked permission to bring him to call, and I consented with alacrity, thinking, as I spoke, that I would, after meeting him, arrange a little dinner-party of choice spirits in his honor.

When we were ready to go, Mrs. D—, to my surprise and embarrassment, did not propose that our hostess should drive down-town with us, although we were going directly back, and a cold "Scotch mist" was beginning to fall. To this day, I do not know to what to attribute what I then felt—what I still consider—was gross incivility. The most charitable supposition is that it never occurred to her that it would be neighborly and humane to offer a luxurious seat in her swiftly rolling chariot to the woman who must otherwise walk a mile in the chill and wet. She had the reputation of absent-mindedness. Let us hope that her wits were off upon an excursion when we got into the carriage and drove away, leaving Mrs. C—at the gate.

Glancing back, uneasily, I saw her raise an umbrella and set out upon her cheerless promenade directly in our wake, and I made a desperate essay at redressing the wrong.

"It is a pity Mrs. C—must go out this afternoon," I said, shiveringly. "She will have a damp walk."

"Yes," assented my companion, readily. "That is the worst of being in this vicinity. There is no street railway within half a mile."

She went no further. I could go no further. The carriage was hers—not mine.

Mrs. C—'s brother did not call on me, nor did she ever again. The latter circumstance might not have excited surprise, had she not treated me with marked coldness when I met her casually at the house of a friend. In the busy whirl of an active life, I should have forgotten this circumstance, or set it down to my own imagination, had not her brother's paper contained, a month or so later, an attack upon myself that amazed me by what I thought was causeless acrimony. Even when I found myself described as rich, haughty and heartless, "consorting with people who could pay visits to me in coaches with monograms upon the doors, and turning the cold shoulder to those who came on foot,"—I did not associate the diatribe with my visit to the writer's relative. Five years afterward, the truth was made known to me by accident. Mrs. C—had judged from something said during our interview that the equipage belonged to me, and that I had brought Mrs. D—to see her instead of being the invited party. I was now a resident of another city. The story came to me by a circuitous route. Explanation was impracticable. Yet it is not six months since there fell under my eye a paragraph penned by the offended brother testifying that his opinion of my insignificant self remains unaltered.

Had he or his sister suspended judgment until the evidence against my ladyhood and humanity could be investigated, I should have had to look elsewhere for an incident with which to point the moral of my Talk.

Rising above the pettiness of spiteful grudge-bearing against a fellow-mortal, let me say a word of the unholy restiveness with which we meet the disappointments which are the Father's discipline of His own. "All these things are against me!" is a cry that has struck upon His loving heart until Godlike patience is needed to bear with the fretful wail.

Nothing that He lets fall upon us can be "against" us! In His hottest fires we have but to "hold still" and bide His good time in order to see that all His purposes in us are mercy, as well as truth to His promises. In the Hereafter deeded to us as a sure heritage, we shall see that each was a part of His design for our best and eternal good.

Marion Harland

CHAPTER XIII

"ACCORDING TO HIS FOLLY."

The hardest task ever set for mortal endeavor is for us to allow other people to know less than we know.

The failure to perform this task has kindled the fagots about the stake where heretics perished for obstinacy.

It is not a week, by the way, since I heard a woman, gently nurtured and intellectual, lament that those "old Pilgrim forefathers were so disagreeably obstinate." She "wondered that their generation did not send them to the scaffold instead of across the sea."

Inability to suffer the rest of the world to be mistaken has set a nation by the ears, broken hearts and fortunes, and separated more chief friends than all other alienating causes combined. Many self-deluding souls set down their impatience with others' errors to a spirit of benevolence. They love their friends too dearly, they have too sincere a desire for the welfare of acquaintances, to let them hold mischievous tenets.

The cause of variance may appear contemptible to an indifferent third party.

To the average reasoner who has no personal concern in the debate, it may seem immaterial at what date Mrs. Jenkyns paid her last visit to Boston. She is positive that it was in March, 1889. Mr. Jenkyns is as certain that she accompanied him thither in April of that year. She establishes her position by the fact that she left her baby for the first time when the cherub was ten months old, and there is the Family Bible to prove that he was born May 10, 1888. Is she likely to be mistaken on such a point when she cried all night in Boston and the bereft infant wailed all night in New York? What does Charles take her for? Hasn't he said, himself, dozens of times, that there is no use arguing as to times and seasons with a woman who verifies these by her children's ages? Mr. Jenkyns has said so—but with a difference. There is no use arguing with a woman in any circumstances, whatsoever. That Emma tries to carry her point now by lugging in the poor little kid, who has nothing whatever to do with the case, is but another proof of the inconsequence of the sex. He has the stub of his check-book to show that he paid the hotel bill in Boston, April 11, 1889. Figures cannot lie. Mrs. Charles Jenkyns challenges the check-book on the spot—and the wrangle goes on until she seeks her chamber to have her cry out, and he storms off to office or club, irritated past forbearance by the pig-headed perversity of a creature he called "angel" with every third breath on their wedding journey to Boston in 1886.

Each of the combatants was confident, after the first exchange of shots, that the other was in error. Half an hour's quarreling left both doubly confident of the truth which was self-evident from the outset. It is sadly probable that neither will ever confess, to himself or to herself, that the only wise course for either to pursue would have been to let ignorance have its perfect work, by abstaining from so much as a hint of contradiction.

"I don't see how you held your temper and your tongue!"

Marion Harland

said one man to another, as a self-satisfied acquaintance strutted away from the pair after a monologue of ten minutes upon a matter of which both of his companions knew infinitely more than he. "I hadn't patience to listen to him, much less answer him good-humoredly—he is such a fool!"

"I let him alone because he is a fool."

"But he is puffed up by the fond impression that you agree with him!"

"That doesn't hurt me,—and waste of cellular tissue in such a cause would!"

"Seest thou a man wise in his own conceit?" asks Solomon. "There is more hope of a fool than of him."

Which I take to mean that self-conceit is the rankest form of folly, a sort of triple armor of defence against counter-statement and rebutting argument. So far as my experience goes to prove a disheartening proposition,—all fools are wise (to themselves) in their own conceit. The first evidence of true wisdom is humility. One may be ignorant without being foolish. Lack of knowledge because the opportunity for acquiring it has been withheld, induces in the human mind such conditions as we find in a sponge that has been cleaned and dried. Information fills and enlarges the pores. Ignorance that is content with itself is turgid and saturated. It will take up no more, no matter what is offered.

This is the form of folly which the preacher admonishes us to answer in kind. The effort to force the truth upon the charged sponge is an exercise of mental muscle akin to the beating of the air, deprecated by the Apostle to the Gentiles.

"Such stolid stupidity is incredible in a land where

education is compulsory!" exclaimed a friend who, having talked himself out of breath in the effort to persuade a rich vulgarian into belief of one of the simplest of philosophical principles, had the mortification of seeing that his opponent actually flattered himself with the idea that *he* had come off victorious in the wordy skirmish. "One would have thought that living where he does, and as he does, he would have taken in such knowledge through the pores."

"Not if the pores were already full," was a retort that shed new light into the educated mind.

Folly has a law and language of its own with which intelligence intermeddles not. The workings of an intellect at once untrained and self-sufficient are like the ways of Infinite Wisdom—past finding out.

Philosophy and politeness harmonize in the effort to meet such intellects upon what they shall not suspect is "made ground." To apply to them the rules of conversation and debate you would use in intercourse with equals would be absurd, and disagreeable alike to you and to themselves. They would never forgive a plain statement of the difference between you and their guild.

As a matter of curious experiment, I made the attempt once, in a case of a handsome dolt, who was, nominally, a domestic in my employ for a few months. She had an affected pose and tread which she conceived to be majestic. She was stupid, awkward and slovenly about her work, and altogether so "impossible" that I disliked to send her adrift upon the world, and was still more averse to imposing her upon another household. In a weak moment I essayed to reason her out of her fatuous vanity, and stimulate in her a desire to make something better of herself. She seemed to hearken while I represented mildly the expediency of learning to do her part in life well and creditably; how

　　　　　Marion Harland

conscience entered into the performance of duties some people considered mean; how, in this country, a washer-woman is as worthy as the President's wife, so long as she respects herself.

Norah's impassive face had not changed, but she interposed here:

"Beg pardon, ma'am! I've no thought of taking a hand with the washing."

I was silly enough to go on with what I had tried to make so plain that the wayfaring "living-out girl" could not err in taking it in. I was willing to train her in the duties of her station. I set forth, and would have specified what these were, but for a second interruption that was evidently not intentionally disrespectful, and was uttered with the bovine stolidity that never forsook her.

"Excuse me, ma'am, but I've always understood that all that made a lady in Ameriky was eddercation, an' shure I have that 's well 's you!"

She could read, or so I suppose, although I never saw a book in her hand, and could probably write, after the fashion of her class.

With a smile at my folly that struggled with a sigh over hers, I let her go. It was my fault not hers, that I had bruised my fists thumping against a stone wall. Had I discoursed to her in Bengalee she would have comprehended me no more imperfectly. The doom of hopelessness was upon her. She was not merely a fool, but had taken the full degree as a self-satisfied blockhead. I deserved what I got—and more of the same sort.

Of a different type—being only a moderately conceited

ignoramus, was an otherwise well-educated woman whom I heard discourse volubly upon ceramics and a valuable collection of old china she had picked up in a foreign town. Among other kinds she named some choice bits of "faience."

"Is not that used now as a general term for earthenware decorated with color?" asked a listener modestly.

"Oh, by no means! It is never applied except to a particular and exceedingly rare sort of pottery," went on the connoisseur. "But perhaps you are not familiar with ceramic terms?"

"Not as familiar as I should be, I confess," rejoined the other, gently regretful.

A couple of years later, I met the enthusiastic collector in the house of the other party to the dialogue, and learned with her that our hostess was renowned for her treasures of old china, and actually the author of a book upon ceramics.

"What must she have thought of me the day I made such a fool of myself!" moaned the humbled woman in a corner to me. "And you know—as I have learned since, as she knew all the time,—that 'faience' is used as a generic term! Well! I have had my lesson in talking of what I do not understand. How could she have answered me so civilly and gravely!"

I was too sorry for her to put into words the thought of the proverbial answer, "according to his folly." The incident had its moral and example for me too. The recollection has beaten back many a vehement protest against egregious absurdity, and helped me endure with apparent composure even the patronage of fools.

After all, there are so many mistakes made by other people

that affect nobody but themselves that Don Quixote might tire of tilting at them. The more asinine the speaker the louder is his bray, and the more surely do we encounter him in social and domestic haunts. To dispute with him is to strengthen the stakes, and twist harder the cords of his belief in himself. In recognizing the truth, so humiliating to human reason, one wonders what effect would be produced by a determined regime of letting alone. Would what St. James graphically describes as "foaming out of their own shame," finally froth itself into silence? Is not the opposition consequent upon the universal desire to set other people right, the breath that blows the flame?

What would be the status of society, what the atmosphere of our homes, were each of us to curb the impulse to controvert doubtful, but important, statements:—to seem to acquiesce in—let us say, in Tom's declaration that there are forty black cats in the back yard, and Polly's opinion that Susie Jones is the prettiest girl in town, when we consider her positively homely, and so on to the end of the day's or week's or month's chapter? If, when we know that a man is a blatant vaporer, we simply let him vapor, and mind our own business; if, having gauged the measure of a woman's mind, and found it only an inch deep, we do not fret our souls by vain dredgings in a channel to-day that will fill up by to-morrow; if we give the fool the benefit of his license; and expend thought and care upon that which is hopeful and profitable—do we not prove ourselves prudent economists of time and labor?

The subject is practical, and merits consideration. In this working-day world of ours there is so much unavoidable pain, and so much annoyance which we cannot overlook, that sensible people cushion corners and shrink aside from brier-pricks. We do ourselves actual physical harm when we lose temper; the tart speech takes virtue out of us. A woman would better fatigue herself by righting an untidy chamber than scold a servant for neglecting it. Foreigners comment surprisedly upon the "anxious faces" of American women even of the better class. The inchoate condition of our domestic service has undoubtedly much to do with the premature seams that mar what would else be fair and sweet, but I incline to the belief that more is due to a certain irritableness which is a national characteristic,—a restless desire to set everything right. The zeal for reform is commendable, but not always according to knowledge. Certain forms of folly cure themselves, if not flattered by grave rebuke, and others do not come within the province of her who has her hands full already. It is easier for us all to find fault than to overlook. It "just drives our woman-reformer wild to hear some people talk!" The least aggressive of us knows for herself the impotent vexation of attempting to convince one who is too dull, or too dogged, to see reason. Why, then, yield to the disposition to attempt the impracticable? If we would live worthily and live long, we must school ourselves in the minor details of self-control and everyday philosophy that make up a useful and well-balanced life.

Marion Harland

CHAPTER XIV

"BUTTERED PARSNIPS."

I shall never forget the first time I heard the homely proverb, once better known than now, "Fine words butter no parsnips."

A bitter-tongued old lady, with an eye like a hawk's, and a certain suspicious turn of the head to this side and that which reminded one of the same bird of prey, was discussing a new neighbor.

"I don't hold with meaching ways at any time and in anybody," said the thin croak, made more husky by snuff, a pinch of which she held between thumb and finger, the joined digits punctuating her strictures. "And she's one of the fair-and-softy sort. A pleasant word to this one, and a smile to that, and always recollecting who is sick, and who is away from home, and ready to talk about what pleases you, and not herself, and praising your biscuits and your bonnets and your babies, and listening to you while you are talking as if there was nobody else upon earth."

Like the octogenarian whose teeth gave out before his dry toast, she "hadn't finished, but she stopped" there, being clean out of breath.

"But Mrs. A.!" I raised my girlish voice to reach the deaf ears. "I think all that is beautiful. I only wish I could imitate her, and be as popular and as much beloved."

"Humph!" inhaling the snuff spitefully. "She's too sweet to be wholesome. Fair words butter no parsnips. Look out for a tongue that's smooth on both sides. What does the Bible say of the hypocrite? 'The words of his mouth were smoother than butter.' I'd rather have honest vinegar!"

I stood too much in dread of her frankness to ask if sugar is never honest, or to speculate audibly why she chose parsnips with their length of fibre and peculiar cloying sweet, as types of daily living. The adage seemed droll enough to me then, and it is odd even now that I have become familiar with it in the talk of old-fashioned people. Interpreting it as they do, I dispute it stoutly. Parsnips may be only passable to most palates even when buttered. They would be intolerable with vinegar. Furthermore,—before we drop the figure,—if anything can butter them, it is fair words.

This business which we call living is not easy at the best. Our parsnips are sometimes tough and stringy; sometimes insipid; often withered by drought or frost-bitten. If served without sauce, they—to quote our old-fashioned people again—"go against the stomach."

There is a pernicious fallacy to the effect that a rough tongue is an honest one. There are quite as many unpleasant untruths told as there are flattering falsehoods. Because a speech is kind it is not of necessity a lie, nor does a remark gain in truth in direct ratio as it loses its politeness. Often the blunt criticism is the outcome of a savage instinct on the part of the perpetrator. In America, men and women (always excepting Italians) do not carry poniards concealed in their breasts, or swords at their sides. In lieu of these the tongue is used to revenge an evil.

The Psalmist exclaims: "Let the righteous smite me; it shall be a kindness; and let him reprove me; it shall be an excellent oil," but the average representative of the nineteenth century will not echo his sentiment. It may be that the "righteous" of that day had a more agreeable way of offering reproof than have the modern saints. However that may be, the "excellent oil" seems to have given place to corrosive sublimate and carbolic acid—neither of which, applied in an undiluted form, may be even remotely suspected of soothing an open wound. True, they are fatal to bacteria, but at the same time they madden the sufferer as would coals of living fire.

Even supposing one lays herself open to the charge of flattery, is it not less of a fault than to merit the reputation for brutal fault-finding? Who would not rather be a healer than a scarifier?

"Faithful may be the wounds of a friend" (and on this word "friend" I lay special stress), but the converse is also true. Faithful are his healings. Have you never had a whole day brightened by some seemingly chance remark which warmed the cockles of your heart with a delicious glow? It may have been that you were disappointed in some cherished scheme—how much disappointed no one guessed and you were ashamed to confess. It may have been that you were struggling to be brave and cheerful under some trial, the weight of which you thought others could not appreciate. The cheering word may only have been—"My dear, how sweet you are looking to-day! You do my old eyes good." Or perhaps an appreciative other-half has pressed your hand and whispered, "You are the bravest little woman in the world!" Who does not remember how, at such a time, the unexpected sympathy or encouragement brought the quick tears to the eyes, and to the cheeks the flush which meant a bound of joy from the heavy heart? If we could but remember that we are told to "speak the truth in love!" In "love," recollect,—not in temper. Do not be the accursed one by whom the offences come. They will come. The Evil One will look out for that, but it is not worth while for you to make his work too easy. Determine to train yourself strictly to see the many excellent qualities possessed by your associates, and you will be surprised to find that before long the disagreeable traits will only appear as foils for the good. Cultivate an eye for pleasant characteristics, and do not encourage people who are prone to rough speech. Frown down the blunt expression of opinion and it will cease to be considered praiseworthy frankness. The woman of whom the Royal Preacher speaks, "in whose tongue was the law of kindness," probably showed that kindness by being agreeable, or we may be sure no human being of the masculine gender would have considered her price far above rubies; nor add with such sublime confidence—"her husband also, and he praises her."

One such woman never forgot to thank anyone for the slightest favor, and I have seen a burly and phlegmatically sombre policeman smile with unexpected pleasure at receiving the sweet-faced "thank you!" with which she always acknowledged his pilotage over a crowded street-crossing.

It is time that people comprehended that it is not their duty to be disagreeably frank, when another's comfort is the price thereof. An unkind sentence has the power of lodgment in the mind. It is like the red "chigoe" which inserts his tiny head in the flesh and burrows until he causes a throbbing fester. For instance, I have never forgotten a speech which was addressed to me over twenty years ago. It was just after we had built an unpretending, but thoroughly cozy summer cottage, nestled in a grove of trees that threw long shadows into a silvery lake. The man in question told me he never saw our light at night from the other side of the pretty sheet of water that it did not "remind him of a charcoal-burner's hut in the heart of a wilderness." It would be of interest to ascertain why this needlessly unkind remark was made. Since there were at least one or two pleasant features in the landscape, why could he not call attention to them?

It is not necessary that we should flatter, but let us be lavishly generous with what French cooks call *sauce agreable*, since parsnips must be eaten. Some efforts in this line remind me of a story I recently heard of a farmer who received at a New York restaurant the customary small pat of butter with his Vienna roll. Imperiously beckoning to a waiter, he commanded him to "wipe that grease spot off that plate, and bring him some butter!"

Let us give more than the grease spot. Better go to the other extreme, and drown our friend's neglected parsnips in fresh, pure un-oleomargarined, and entirely sweet butter.

CHAPTER XV

IS MARRIAGE REFORMATORY?

To no other estate are there so many varieties of phases as to that of matrimony. Like the music of Saint Caecilia and old Timotheus combined, it is capable of raising "a mortal to the skies," or of bringing "an angel down" to the lowest depths of misery. At the best the betrothed couple can never say with absolute certainty—"After marriage we shall be happy." The experience of wedded life is alarmingly like that of dying—each man and woman must know it for himself and herself, and no other human being can share its trials or its joys.

The mistake the prospective wife makes is in obstinately closing her eyes to the fact that married life has any trials which are not far outbalanced by its pleasures. Marriage does not change man or woman. The impressive ceremony over, the bridal finery laid aside, the last strain of the wedding-march wafted into space, and the orange-flowers dead and scentless,—John becomes once more plain, everyday John, with the same good traits which first won his Mary's heart, and the many disagreeable characteristics that exasperated his mother and sisters. And Mary, being a woman, and no more of a saint than is her life-partner, will also be exasperated. If John is an honest gentleman who loves Mary, the chances for her happiness depend upon her

Marion Harland

common-sense and her love for John. It is utterly impossible to have too much of the last-named commodity. It will be all needed, well-blended with the divine attribute of patience, and judiciously seasoned with woman's especial gift—tact, to enable man and wife to live together peaceably for one year.

Moreover, Mary must understand that John the lover and John the husband have very different ways of showing affection. The lover would loiter evening after evening waiting for other guests to go home that he might have time for a few tender words with his sweetheart. Woman's logic reasons,—"what more natural when he has hours of time than for him to keep on saying those same tender words, only very many more of them?" The fact remains that he does not. After the kiss of welcome on his arrival home at the close of day, he is unsentimental enough to want his dinner, and, that disposed of, he buries himself behind his newspaper, from which perhaps he does not emerge before nine o'clock when he is ready to talk to Mary and to be entertained by her.

And yet this John of whom I am talking is as good morally, as faithful and conscientious in his manly way as Mary in her womanly.

But—suppose he were not a good man, what then? Could the mere fact of his union with her change his entire nature?

A good man may be made better by association with a good woman; a man with repressed evil tendencies may have them held more firmly in check by his wife's restraining influence, but no woman should undertake to "make over" a man who has given way to the wicked passions of his being until they are beyond his control. He will not be made a reputable member of society and a bright and shining light to the community in which he dwells, by marrying. He does not go into the new life as a sort of Keeley cure,—a reformatory institution. A woman's strongest and weakest point is her power of idealizing every cold fact with which she comes in contact. She loves a handsome roue. He tells her that if she will but take him in training she can make a new man of him; that her fair hand can wipe all the dark spots from his past life, smooth the rough places and elevate the depressions in his character until it will be once more goodly to contemplate. And over the stereopticon view of the man his fiancee throws the rosecolored light of her idealistic lantern, and believes all he says. Of course during their engagement he frequently slips back into the old path, sometimes has a downfall that shocks and horrifies her who would reform him, but, once more trimming and turning up the wick, she bathes him in the pink light and remembers that he is not yet as entirely under her influence as he will be some day. She would think it cruel injustice were some unprejudiced observer to suggest that if he cannot change his life when the possibilities of winning her are at stake, he will hardly do so when the prize is his own.

It is doubtful if a man whose whole nature has become stunted, warped and foul by sin, has in him the ability to love a true woman as she deserves to be loved. I do not mean to intimate that his devotion to her is feigned, but it is only such attachment as he is capable of, and is no more to be compared with the unselfish love that she freely lavishes upon him, than the mud-begrimed slush which settles in city gutters to the snowy blanket covering country fields.

Beauty and the Beast may be a pretty fairy-tale, but in the realism of practical life it assumes the guise of a tragedy that makes the looker-on shudder with disgustful pity. My heart aches when I think of the women who began the work of reformation with hope and laid it down with despair at the end of a life that made them "turn weary arms to death"

Marion Harland

with a sigh of welcome. On the table before me stands the portrait of one such woman. When she was a merry-hearted girl, she fell in love with a handsome, brilliant young fellow, whose only failing was a dangerous fondness for liquor. He loved her deeply—better than anything else in the world—except drink. Nevertheless, he promised to overcome even this passion for her sake. During the month immediately preceding their marriage, he came twice into her presence intoxicated. In vain did her family plead and protest. Her only answer was:

"Harry cannot keep straight without some one to help him. I must marry him now. He needs me!"

Two years after her marriage she died of a broken heart, whispering at the last to a dear friend that she "was not sorry to go, but would be thankful life was over if she were only sure that her year-old baby would not be left to Harry's care."

Yet he was in most respects tender and considerate. The trouble was that his devotion to her remained at the point at which it stood when he became her husband. The habit of intemperance grew.

Suppose that, added to this great fault, had been others still more vicious. Had his been a coarse brutal nature, would not the idea of reformation have been still more hopeless?

A woman, in tying herself for life to an unprincipled man who has yielded to the dictates of sin year after year, forgets that he has lost to a great extent his better nature and is now hardly responsible for his actions. The spirit may indeed be willing, but the flesh is lamentably weak. The appetites that have been long indulged do not relinquish their claims after only a few months' restraint, and when the girl for whose sake they have been repressed is won, they will return to the swept and garnished room, and the last end of their victim will be worse than the first.

I often wonder what a good, pure woman promises herself when she proposes to entwine her clean life with one that is scarred, seamed and blackened. Evade the truth as she may, there are but two courses for her to pursue. She must either live a lonely life apart from her husband's, frowning down, or silently showing disapproval of his habits, or she must, to preserve peace and the semblance of happiness, bring herself down to his level and become even less delicate and more degraded than he. For is not a coarse woman always more abhorrent than a coarse man? There are the instincts of her entire moral and physical nature to be cast aside before she can descend to vulgarity. In the one case her husband will hate her, while in the other she will lose his respect and will despise herself.

An evil life so blunts the conscience that the wife of an unreformed man need hardly expect him to be faithful to her. If a man will sin against common decency, morality and social codes, he will sin against his wife.

There is another aspect of the case to be considered. The American girl of to-day seldom takes the possibility of offspring into her matrimonial plans. They are not only a possibility, but a probability, and it behooves every woman to cast aside false modesty, and with a pure heart and honest soul seriously consider if she is not doing irreparable wrong to unborn children in giving them an unprincipled father. Is she willing to see her children's blood tainted by his vices, their lives wrecked by evil temptations inherited from him? She must, indeed, be a reckless woman and a soulless, who, with this thought uppermost can still say, "I will marry this man—let the consequences be what they may!"

That a man has some redeeming qualities does not make

him a life-companion to be desired above all others. Said a poor Irish woman:

"Pat is always a good husband, savin' the toimes he's in liquor!"

"When is he sober?" asked a bystander.

"Sure an' his money gin'rally gives out by Friday mornin', and from that on to Saturday night, he can't git a dhrop. Faith, but he's koind and consid'rate at sich a time!"

Did the loyal soul find that marriage paid?

One great mistake that many silly women make is to think that a dash of wickedness makes a man more attractive. Years ago I heard a girl say:

"I want to know Jack S. He has been very wild, and a man is so much more interesting for being a little naughty, you know."

I did not "know," nor do I now understand why pearls should plead to be thrown before swine, or fresh-blown roses upon the dung-hill.

CHAPTER XVI

"JOHN'S" MOTHER

One of the oldest problems among the many seemingly contradictory "examples" set for the student of human nature has to do with the different positions assigned to mother and mother-in-law.

Painters, poets, divines, sages,—the inspired Word itself,—rank the mother's office as the noblest assigned to creatures of mortal mould. Mother-love and the love of the dear Father of us all are compared, the one with the other. Of all human affections, this, the first that takes root in the infant's heart, is the last to die out under the blighting influence of vice, the deadening blows of time. "My Mother" is spoken by the world-hardened citizen with a gentler inflection,—a reverential cadence, as if the inner man stood with uncovered head before a shrine.

Mother-in-law! The words call a smile that is too often a sneer to lips in which dwells habitually the law of kindness, while lampoon, caricature, jest and song find in them theme and catchword for mockery and insult.

I witnessed, not long ago, the skillful impersonation of a husband who held in his hand a letter just received from his wife. The first page informed him that after his departure from home his wife's mother had arrived; the second, that she intended to remain during the winter; the third, that she had been taken suddenly and violently ill; and the fourth, that she was dead. The reader spoke no word while perusing the epistle, but his facial play attested his emotions better than speech could have done. His countenance was grave on learning of the visit, desperate at the thought of its length, and expressed annoyance at the inconvenience of her illness while under his roof; when the final page was reached, his features became illumined with ecstatic joy. Dropping the letter, he clasped his hands, and, raising his eyes, ejaculated with blissful fervor—

"Thank Heaven! she's dead!"

Of course we laughed. It was expected of us. Nevertheless, this kind of jesting has its effect. It is dangerous playing with edged tools that would be better laid aside and allowed to rust instead of being brought forward where they may do mischief.

The relation of mother-in-law and son-or daughter-in-law ought to be what I am glad to think it sometimes is, one of perfect harmony. The mother who has brought up a daughter to woman's estate, and made her fit to be the wife of a good man and the mother of his children, should be appreciated by the man who profits by the wife's mother's teachings. Had this mother been careless and negligent, allowing the daughter to cultivate traits that make her husband wretched, how quick would he be to lay the blame where it belongs,—upon the mother who trained, or left untrained the daughter. Why should he not give credit to the same source?

There are many women who, to their shame be it said, openly sneer at their mothers-in-law, and ridicule their manners, habits, etc. Yet, in the same breath, the woman of this class will freely state that she has "the best husband in all creation." Whose influence made him the man he is, if not the mother's with whom, for so many years, he was the first and dearest care, until she uncomplainingly saw him leave her home with the girl he married?

Husband and wife do not look into the matter deeply enough to think what underlies this dislike for the other's mother. The man who truly loves his wife will do all in his power and make any self-sacrifice to further her happiness. If she is not an exceptional woman, she will be made happier by his affection for the mother to whom she is devoted, and miserable by a lack of this sentiment. Let us argue the case according to rule. It makes Mary happy if John is fond of her mother, and unhappy if he is not. If John loves Mary he wishes to make her happy. *Ergo*, when he shows his love for her mother he is likewise giving evidence of his love for Mary.

So, when I hear a so-called devoted wife cast unkind slurs upon her mother-in-law, I wonder how genuine is the affection for her husband which allows her to make him unhappy by awaking in his breast suspicions that his mother is distasteful to his wife. True love would hardly be so cruel. What if John's mother has disagreeable peculiarities? She is none the less his mother, and, as such, he is bound to love and respect her. If the love he bears her blinds him to her deficiencies, is it not the part of a true wife to keep his eyes closed to these foibles, since seeing them will make him uncomfortable? Every man likes to feel that his dear mother and dearer wife are congenial friends. And it is their duty to be friendly, if not congenial.

The mother-in-law, too, has her task. It would be folly to state that she is not often and grossly to blame for the uncomfortable state of this relationship. She is frequently a trifle jealous, sometimes fails to remember how she felt when young, resents her child's love for, and dependence on, another, feels bitterly that she no longer has it in her power to make her darling's happiness, and has such a high ideal of what should be the qualities of the partner her girl has chosen that she puts his faults under a magnifying glass of criticism until the molehills become mountains, and appreciation of the good is swallowed up in recognition of every evil trait. Happily, this is not always the case, and the genuine mother is, as a rule, so grateful to see her child happy that for his or her sake she loves the one who causes this contentment, even if he or she be far from congenial to herself, and "not the man she would have picked out for her daughter to marry."

I have serious doubts as to whether the existing antagonism would have been half so prevalent had not such a multitude of coarse jokes been perpetrated on the subject. The best way to perpetuate an evil is to take it for granted and to speak of it as a matter of course. I am glad to be able to name among my friends more than one man who is large-souled enough to tenderly love and respect his wife's mother, and several women who frankly acknowledge that their own special mothers-in-law are all goodness and kindness.

It is natural that people brought up differently, and living separately for a long term of years, should, when thrown into close relationship, differ on many subjects, and clash in various opinions, and that occasional misunderstandings should arise. Even with husband and wife this is true. But if man and woman can, for the affection they bear each other, forgive and forget these little differences, why may not each, for the same sweet love's sake, and in the thought of what maternal devotion is, pardon and overlook the foibles of the other's mother?

One evil effect of pasquinade and sneer is to put the

prospective daughter-in-law on the defensive, and prepare her mind, unconsciously to herself, to regard her future husband's mother as her natural enemy. Many a girl marries with the preconceived notion that, to preserve her individual rights, and to rule in her own small household, she must carefully guard against the machinations of the much-decried mother-in-law. Nine times out of ten, had not this thought become slowly but securely rooted in past years, the intercourse between the two women might be all peace and harmony. The young wife's mind is, insensibly to her, poisoned before she enters the dreaded relation (in law). She is on the alert, defensive, ready to impute motives to the mother-in-law she would never dream of attributing to her own parent, in like circumstances.

Yet, many a girl has never known what maternal love means until at her marriage she was welcomed by the open arms and large heart of her husband's mother. It is not only orphan girls who have this experience, for some parents never bestow upon their children the peculiar brooding tenderness which all young people need, even when they have almost attained man's and woman's estate. Said one youthful matron to me—"My own mother has been an invalid for so many years that I have not felt that I could go to her with all my worries and perplexities, for my annoyances only added to her troubles. Therefore, never until I was married did I know what real "mothering" meant. Then my husband's mother seemed as much mine as his. I was her "daughter." When my first baby was coming, all the dainty little garments were furnished by this grandmamma, and her care and tenderness for me were such that the remembrance of them fills my heart to overflowing with gratitude." Another woman told me with a moved smile that she was "so fortunate a woman as to have two mothers," while a man I know openly declares that his mother-in-law is "the best mother in the world,—next to his own mother."

Marion Harland

One elderly woman, who has been a mother-in-law five times, informed me the other day that in her heart she knew little difference between her own daughters and sons and their respective husbands and wives. "You see," she said, "they are all my dear children."

I cite these instances merely to prove how happily harmonious this oft-abused state may be, and what a pity it is that it should ever be otherwise.

If you, my reader, do not enjoy the relationship, allow me to suggest a cure for the trouble. Put your own mother—or daughter—in the place of the offender, and act according to the light thrown upon the subject by this shifting of positions. Say to yourself—"This woman means well, but she does not know me yet well enough to understand just how to put things in the way to which I have been accustomed. She loves John so well that she seems unjust or inconsiderate to me. She could not, in the eyes of John's wife, have a better excuse for hasty speech or harsh action."

The love you both bear this same oft-perplexed John should be at once solvent and cement, melting hardness, and uniting seemingly antagonistic elements.

Above all things, as John's wife, never criticise his mother to him. If he sympathizes with you, he is disloyal to his mother; if not, you consider him unfeeling, and imme-diately accuse him of "taking sides" against you. Think for one moment of your own boy, perhaps still a mere baby. Does it not, even now, grieve you to the heart to think that the day will come when he will discuss and acknowledge your faults to anyone, albeit his listener is only his wife? If John is the man he should be, he fancies that his mother is "a creature all too bright and good" to be criticised, and, as you want your son to have the same opinion of his mother, uphold John in his fealty, and scorn to destroy such blessed love and faith. Make the effort to see John's mother with his eyes, and by so doing make him love you better, and prove yourself worthy to be the wife of a true man and the mother of a son who will be as leal and steadfast as his father.

CHAPTER XVII

AND OTHER RELATIONS-IN-LAW

The other day I chanced to be a listener to the conversation of two young married women. They were making their plans for the coming week. One of them remarked, drearily:

"Henry's sister and her husband are to spend next Sunday with me."

"Are they!" exclaimed the other. "And my husband's father and mother are to honor me by a visit on the same day."

For a moment there was silence, then No. 1 said in an awed voice:

"My dear, you and I need the prayers of the congregation. We are both objects of pity. Our relations-in-law are upon us!"

Within my secret self I pondered whether or not the visitors dreaded the expected ordeal as much as the visited did.

The phrases, "my husband's relatives," "my wife's family," are seldom pronounced without an accompanying bitter thought. John tolerates Mary's kin, and Mary regards John's father and mother, sisters and brothers with an ill-concealed distrust and enmity. Sometimes there is just cause for this antagonistic feeling; more frequently it is the outcome of custom. It is fashionable to regard connections by marriage as necessary evils. Some families, resolved to make the best of that which is inevitable, put a smiling face upon the whole matter, and hide from the outside world the knowledge of their chagrin. No mother has ever seen the girl she thought quite good enough for her boy whom she considers the model of all that is noble and manly, while that sister is rare who feels that the wife chosen by her favorite brother is what "the dear boy really needs as a life-long companion." Once in a great while, when the chosen bride by some remarkable chance happens to suit the family fancy, the whole world is informed of the fact, and the bride elect inwardly pronounces John's blood relations to be "awfully gushing" or "desperately hypocritical." The happy medium is difficult of attainment.

Of course there are some exceptions to the general rule of antagonism. And I am glad to believe that sometimes, even when this feeling exists, husband and wife are too considerate of one another's comforts to betray any sign of discontent. Said a woman to me:

"My dear, Mrs. S. is John's mother, and it is my duty to conceal from him the fact that she is disagreeable to me. I could be a much happier woman for never seeing my mother-in-law again, but my husband must never suspect it. The dear fellow flatters himself that his wife and mother 'hit it off so well together.' To our credit be it said, that we have never enlightened him as to the true state of affairs."

And for the sake of the man they both loved, these women refrained from outward evidence of the intense dislike each felt for the other.

The trouble begins very far back. When the boy is

laughingly warned against "the girl with a family," and the girl is reminded that this or that jolly fellow "has a dragon of a mother," the evil seed is sown. From that time until the pair are forever united at the altar, it grows, and with marriage it begins to bring forth the unpeaceable fruits of endless dissensions. I sometimes wonder if the new life could be begun with a predisposition towards amity, what the result would be.

There is fault on both sides from the beginning. It is an accepted proverb that no house is large enough to hold two families, and certainly no family is large enough to contain two factions. As soon as the son of the household marries, an antagonistic element is introduced. Mother and sisters immediately bring to bear upon the new bride opera-glasses of criticism,—viewing faults through the small end, and virtues through the large.

It would be strange indeed if two women who have never met until the younger one was of a marriageable age, should have the same methods of housekeeping, etc. But the mother-in-law is inclined to believe that John's wife should do things her way, and that any other way is slovenly, new-fangled, or ridiculous. The son's wife—possessing her share of individuality—resents the interference, and shows that resentment. Too often, alas! both make the dreary mistake of retailing their sorrows to John, and then the breach becomes too wide ever to be bridged over. Unless John is an exceptionally independent man he will attempt in his clumsy way to bring both women to the same way of thinking, and the result would be ludicrous were it not also pitiful. The chances are nine hundred and ninety-nine to one thousand that he will succeed in making his mother feel that he is unduly influenced by his silly wife, while said wife thinks indignantly that John is, and always will be, "under his mother's thumb."

I firmly believe that Mary is often to blame for John's dislike for her family. When she marries, she revels in the new and delightful sensation of having some one to "take her part," and sympathize with her in all her petty annoyances and big troubles. Her father, mother, sisters and brothers often vex her, and what more natural than that she should pour her tale of woe into the young husband's ears? He is delightfully indignant and full of pity for her and resentment towards those who have caused her discomfort. At all events he understands her!

By the time the story is told and she is duly consoled she has forgotten her injuries. She loves her family, and while they are sometimes very trying, who could expect her to bear a grudge against the dear ones? The little burst of anger over, she feels towards them as she has always felt and banishes from her mind all thought of the little occurrence.

Not so, John! His wife (and the possessive pronoun casts about her an atmosphere of importance) has been made uncomfortable, and he is up in arms. His and no one's else is the right to criticise Mary. What business have these people to interfere? He immediately becomes his wife's most ardent champion, and while he muses the fire burns, until he is ready to take the poor little woman away from all her inconsiderate relatives. What is his chagrin on discovering that the woman who, but a few hours ago sobbed out to him her wrongs, has seemingly overlooked all injuries, and is just as fond of sister and brother, and quite as dependent upon "Papa and Mamma" as she ever was. In vain he protests and calls to her mind their injustice. Yes, she remembers it, now that he speaks of it, but the dear people meant nothing unkind, they love her dearly at heart. For her part she could not take to heart a little thing like that. And John remarks that if she is mean-spirited enough to pass by such an occurrence, he has nothing to say. It is her family, thank goodness, not his! After this, he is more quick than ever before to detect a fancied slight and to resent it. Mary laments secretly that "John does not love her family." It is a genuine grief to her, and she does not appreciate the fact that she herself began the work that has now gone too far to check.

Were I to give a piece of advice to a bride, it would be— Never complain to your husband of the actions of a single member of your family, and never find fault with *his* nearest of kin. Your liege lord may disapprove of the members of his own family, or perhaps of some of his mother's characteristics, and he may talk to you of them. But he will hotly resent your mention of them, and will exercise all his masculine ingenuity to prove that his relatives always mean to act for the best,—exactly what you would have him believe of your nearest and dearest. A woman who has never had a suspicion of difference with her relations-in-law, confides to me of the course she has pursued throughout her married life. She says:

"I have never told Charlie that I notice the faults of his family, nor have I ever called his attention to any of their foibles. In that way I have prevented him from feeling that he must side with them against me. He comes to me often with the story of some difference he has had with his mother, and he talks freely of his sister's failings and his brother's inconsistencies. He even sometimes gets righteously indignant, and fairly sputters. Inwardly, I chuckle with amusement, and outwardly I appear sympathetic, but never a word do I say to commit myself. It is his family, and if there is a row, I, to quote Young America, 'am not in it.'"

I happen to know that this woman's husband's family think that "Charlie has a none-such of a wife," and that they are all fond of her.

If tact and diplomacy are ever exercised, it must be in the

management of relations-in-law. The thought that so often the state is one of hatred, or, at best, tolerance, makes the position of all concerned strained and delicate. To many a mother the term "mother-in-law" is a much-dreaded appellation. A woman upon whom this doubtful honor has recently been laid, said to me:

"I hope my boy will never set his wife against me by asking her to 'do things as his mother did.' I shudder to think of it. I want him to tell her that the mince and pumpkin pies, biscuits, muffins, and even gingerbread, made by his wife are vastly superior to any ever produced by his mother. I would rather take the second place in my son's affections than have my new daughter for one moment think of me as her 'mother-in-law.'"

I believe that this is the sincere sentiment of more than one fond mother, as I am also sure that many a fond wife would rather have her husband loved by her own family than to receive so much affection herself. She is sure of her position, but John is a dreadful "relation-in-law," and it is hard to love such. It is sad to think such a mother or wife makes a fatal mistake from the very start, and herself brings about the state of affairs she dreads.

The recognition of a fact often seems to make it doubly true. The knowledge that relations-in-law are frequently relations-at-war, predisposes both parties to unjust judgment. Did each determine to see all the good possible in the other, connections-by-marriage might become kin-at-heart.

CHAPTER XVIII

A TIMID WORD FOR THE STEP-MOTHER

At a luncheon party of a dozen women which I attended last winter, this very topic was introduced. Strangely enough, there were present three women whose mothers had died while the children were still infants, and whose fathers had married again, and two women who were themselves step-mothers. Each of the three who could not remember her own mother agreed that she who took her place had filled it so conscientiously that the child hardly felt the lack. The two step-mothers confessed that they loved their husbands' children as dearly as their own. Said one woman:

"When people speak to me of my step-daughter I have to stop and think which one of the children I did not bring into the world. She is as dear to me as my own flesh and blood."

After we had gleaned all the evidence of truth from the chaff to which we are sometimes treated, a lively member of the company remarked ruefully:

"I declare, all that I have just heard makes me positively ashamed that I did not have a step-mother, or that there is no prospect as far as I can see into the dim future, of my ever becoming one."

There is something to be said on both sides, and we may as well face the facts without prejudice. No woman, however tender, can really take an own mother's place. Her step-children may think that she does, and this is one of the instances where ignorance is such genuine bliss that it would be cruel folly to enlighten it. It would not be natural if actual mother-love could be felt by a woman toward any children save those for whom she has braved the danger of death and the mightiest pain mortal can know. With this suffering comes a love far greater than the anguish, a passionate devotion which, we are certain, must reach beyond the grave itself. That mother who, having young children, still wishes to die, is an anomaly rarely met with. No matter how much she may be forced to endure, she still prays to live for her sons' and daughters' sakes. A poor sufferer once said:

"If I had no child I would beg the good Lord to let me die. But while my baby lives, I beg Him to spare this life which is too valuable to Him to be lost."

It is not possible that an outsider "whose own the sheep are not" should know this heaven-given feeling. Still, every unselfish mother will acknowledge that were she dying, she would be comforted to know that her children would find some conscientious, true foster-mother who would bring them up just as faithfully and tenderly as she knew how to do.

There is no more forlorn being on this wide earth than a widower with little children, and with no woman-relative to help him look after them. Why then this rooted hatred and horror of step-mothers?

You—my step-mother reader—are sadly unfortunate if anyone has been so cruel to you and your charges as to instil into their minds an aversion for you with whom they must live for years, perhaps all their lives. But, perhaps, after all, the case is not so bad as you fear. You may have a morbid sensitiveness on the subject which makes it look very dark to you. Even if matters are as you think, if you try conscientiously to overcome the children's prejudice, and your husband aids you in your efforts, you are bound to live down their dislike. Children are tender-hearted and clear-sighted. They will soon judge for themselves, and the one rule against which they will not rebel is that of love. The first thing for you to do is to begin with your own feelings. *Make* yourself love the little ones. Unless they are unusually unattractive the task will not be a difficult one. Perhaps you love them already. If so, half the battle is won. In driving a restless horse, it is absolutely essential that you should not be at all nervous yourself. Every horseman will tell you that the animal knows instinctively the character of the person managing him. If a thrill of fear touches him who holds the reins, the horse responds to it as to an electric shock, and becomes almost beside himself with nervousness. If a firm, steady, yet gentle grasp is on the lines, the creature obeys in spite of himself. This same principle applies to children. If you cannot control yourself the children know it, and you may as well give up all idea of curbing them. The nervous twitching at the bit and the attempt to govern them by reason of your superior age or knowledge aggravates the evil. It is a mistake to forget that children are human beings, with sensitive feelings like our own, only not as hardened and used to the ways of this unsympathetic world as we are. Their government must have love at its beginning, continuing and ending if it would be successful.

You may as well recognize the fact first as last that you are laboring under a disadvantage in that the hyphenized "step" must precede your name of mother. This being the case, you have need to add to your love patience, and to that tact, and to that pity. If the children exasperate you, do not let them guess it. Keep a rigid guard upon the harsh tongue. If the demon of Impatience tempts you to utter the quick "Stop that noise!" or "Do be quiet!"—seal your lips as surely as if life and death depended upon your silence. Your most severe critics will not be slow in discovering that you love them too much to "scold" or be cross. You make tremendous strides towards their love when they cannot point to a single unjust act that you commit against them.

It may be well in passing to remind you that boys and girls remember an injustice for many years. They themselves are often fair enough to acknowledge after the first flush of anger is over, that they merited a punishment which they have received. As a rule, until they are old men and women, they do not forget the undeserved blow, the unprovoked sarcasm. We many times receive patiently, as grown men and women, reminders that we are doing wrong, but we find it hard to pardon the person who accuses us falsely.

The most powerful auxiliary love can have in accomplishing its end is tact. Some people have more than others, but at all times it may be cultivated. Perhaps the best rule by which to learn it is the old one of "Put yourself in his place." Reverse the positions as in Anstey's "Vice Versa," and imagine yourself a hot-headed, sore-hearted, prejudiced child, with a step-mother against whom your mind has been poisoned by those older and presumably wiser than yourself. How would you receive this or that correction? Acquire the habit of thus putting the matter before your mind's eye, and you will soon find that tactful patience becomes second nature.

If you can possibly avoid it, do not correct the children in the presence of other people, or complain to their father of them. If he once reproves them with the prefix, "Your mother tells me that you have done so-and-so," he has laid the foundations of a distrust difficult to remove. Rather let them domineer over you than try to manage them by appealing to their father, and, thus making them feel sure that you are attempting to prejudice him against them. They are naturally suspicious, and it will take very little to make them positively certain that you are their natural enemy.

Never fail to remember the great and irreparable loss which these children have suffered in the death of the only person in the wide world who could thoroughly understand them. If you had a mother to help you in your childhood, you will know what they miss, or, if you, too, were a lonely little being, let the memory of that loneliness make you lovingly pitiful towards the children who suffer in the same way. Such pity soon leads to an unconquerable love.

Bear in mind in justification of what may seem like unreasonable prejudice, that all children have heard many stories, some of which are true, of the cruelties of step-parents. Doubtless, you in your own life, have known of more than one second wife who was jealous of her husband's love for the first wife's children. When women are heartless they are desperately cruel, and do not hesitate to vent their hatred upon the little ones whose look, Mrs. Browning tells us,—

"is dread to see,
For they mind you of their angels in high places,
With eyes turned on Deity."

She also reminds those whose consciences are so hardened by selfishness that they dare be cruel to the mere babies in their care that—

"The child's sob in the darkness curses deeper Than the strong man in his wrath."

We have not to do in this Talk with this type of woman, but with beings of the mother-sex who would, if they were allowed, make life brighter for the bereaved little ones.

One way to keep step-children's affection is to talk to them often and reverently of their own mother. This is due to them and to her who bare them. Do not allow them to forget her, and guard against the entrance of any jealous feeling into this sacred duty of keeping her memory fresh. The children were hers, and in the eternal home will be hers again. They are only lent to you as a sacred trust. It is not sacrilegious to believe that their mother knows of your efforts to make them good men and women, and that she, as their guardian angel, will not forget to bless her who gives her life to the children who were once "the sweetest flowers" her own "bosom ever bore."

CHAPTER XIX

CHILDREN AS HELPERS

A correspondent inquires whether or not children ought to be trained to do housework and to make themselves useful in the numerous ways in which the young hands and feet can save the older ones.

Unless you expect to be a millionaire many times over, and in perpetuity—emphatically Yes!

It is not necessary that your little daughter should become a drudge; that she should have imposed upon her tasks beyond her strength, or which interfere with out-door exercise and merry in-door play. But through all her childhood must be borne in mind the fact that she is now in training for womanhood, that should she ever marry and have a home of her own, the weight of unaccustomed household tasks will bend and bruise the shoulders totally unaccustomed to burdens of any kind.

If you have a colt that in years to come you intend using as a carriage-horse, you will not let him stand idle in the stable eating and fattening until he is old enough for your purpose. He would then be, in horse-parlance, so "soft" that the lightest loads would weary and injure him. Instead of that, while still young, he is frequently exercised, and broken in, judiciously, first to the harness, then to draw a light vehicle, and so on, until he himself does not know when the training ceases and the actual work begins.

The college-boy, looking forward to "joining the crew," trains for months beforehand, walking, running, rowing, until the flaccid muscles become as firm and hard as steel.

In America, where fortunes are made, lost, and made and lost again in a day, we can never say confidently that our children will inherit so much money that it will always be unnecessary for them to work. And, even could we be sure that our daughters will marry wealthy men, we should, for their own happiness and comfort, teach them that there is work for everyone in this world, and certain duties which every man and woman should perform in order to preserve his or her self-respect.

By the time your child can walk, he may begin to make himself useful. One little boy, three years old, finds his chief delight in "helping mamma." He has his own "baby duster" with which he assiduously rubs the rungs of the parlor chairs until his little face beams with the proud certainty that he is of some use to humanity, and that "dear mamma" could not possibly have dusted that room without her little helper. He brings her boots and gloves when she is preparing for a walk, and begs to be allowed to put her slippers on her feet when she returns home. Often when she is writing and he has grown weary of play, the tender treble asks,—

"Dear Mamma, you are vewy busy. Can't I help you?"

Of course it is an interruption, and he cannot be of the least assistance; but is not that request better than the fretful whine of the child who is sated with play and still demands more?

Marion Harland

"She missed the little *hindering* thing."

says one line of a heart-breaking old poem descriptive of a bereaved mother's loneliness.

Eugene Field strikes the same chord, until she who has laid a child under the sod thrills with remorseful pain:

"No bairn let hold until her gown,
Nor played upon the floore,—
Godde's was the joy; a lyttle boy
Ben in the way no more!"

Ah, impatient mother! as you put aside the affectionate officiousness of the would-be assistant, with frown or hasty word, bethink yourself for one moment of the possible time when, in the dreary calm of a well-ordered house, you will hearken vainly for shrilly-sweet prattle and pattering feet!

There are ways in which even the toddlers can make work lighter for the mothers. When your small daughter has finished with her toys, she should be obliged to put them away in a box kept for that purpose. The mother and nurse will thus be spared the bending of the back and stooping of the knees to accomplish this light task, and the child will enjoy the occupation, and feel very important and "grown-up" in putting her doll to bed, and dolly's furniture, clothes, etc., in their proper place.

When making the beds, allow the little girl to hand you the pillows; and, even should you stumble over her and them, sometimes, you will do well to maintain the pious pretence that she lightens your work by assisting in tucking in the covers, and in gathering up soiled articles of clothing and putting them in the clothes-bag or hamper. She will soon learn to dust chair-rungs and legs, and to wipe off the base-board,—and do it more conscientiously than hireling

Abigail. She may pick bits of thread, string and paper from the carpet, and clean door-handles and window-sills. One mother, when making pies, places her four-year old daughter in a chair at the far end of the kitchen table, and gives her a morsel of dough and a tiny pan. The little one watches the mother and attempts to handle her portion of pastry as mamma does. After it is kneaded, it is tenderly deposited, oftentimes a grayish lump, in spite of carefully washed hands (for little hands will somehow get dirty, try sedulously though you and their owner may to prevent it), in the small tin, and it is placed in the oven with the other pies. It serves admirably at a doll's tea-party, and the meddlesome fingers have been kept busy, the restless mind contented, while the housewife's work is accomplished.

By the time your girl is ten years old, she should be equal to making her own bed, some older person turning the mattresses for her that the young back may not be strained by lifting, and to dust and keep her own little room in order. Of course you will have to watch carefully, and teach her little by little, line upon line. A model housekeeper used to say that one should "cultivate an eye for dirt." Bear this in mind, and cultivate your daughter's eye for dust, dirt and cobwebs. You will find, unless she is a phenomenal exception to the majority of young people, that she will not see when the soap-cup needs washing, or that there are finger-smears on the doors, and "fluff" in the corners. But with the blessed mother-gift of patience, point out to her, again and again, the seemingly small details, the "hall-marks" of housewifery, which, heeded, make the thrifty, neat housekeeper, and, when neglected, the slattern. As she grows older, let her straighten the parlors every morning, make the cake on Saturdays, and show her that you regard her as your right-hand woman in all matters pertaining to domestic affairs. Give her early to understand that it is to her interest to keep her father's house looking neat, that it is her home, and reflects credit, or the reverse, upon herself, and that it is her duty, and should be her pleasure, to help you, her mother, when you are overwearied and need rest. She will enjoy play as a child, society and recreation as a girl, all the more because she has some stated tasks. She may learn to manage the family mending by aiding you in sorting and repairing the clothes when they come up from the wash. When she is capable of entirely relieving you of this burden, pay her a stated amount each week for doing it. She will glory in the delightful feeling of independence imparted by the knowledge of her ability to earn her own pocket-money, and take the first lesson in that much-neglected branch of education,—knowledge of the value of dollars and cents, and how to take care of them.

Few children are born with a sensitive conscience regarding their work, so the mother will, at first, find it necessary to keep an eye on all the tasks performed by the willing, if often careless, girl. Do not judge her too harshly. Try to recall how you felt when you were a lazy, because a rapidly growing, girl; bear in mind that it is natural for kittens and all young creatures to be careless and giddy, and try to be gentle and forbearing while correcting and training her. If she is good for anything, your care will be rewarded in years to come by seeing her trying to do all her work in life "as mamma does."

While it is especially expedient that the girls receive this domestic training, the boys of the family should not be exempt from their share of the responsibility. You need not dread that this kind of work will make your boy unmanly or effeminate. It will rather teach him to be more considerate of women, more appreciative of the amount that his mother and sisters have to do, and less careless in imposing needless labor upon them.

Some mothers go so far as to instruct their sons in the delicate tasks of darning stockings, and repairing rents in their own clothes. There is a vast difference in the skill manifested by different boys. Some seem to have a natural aptitude for dainty work while others have fingers that are "all thumbs." One man, now a father, cherishes a tiny cushion of worsted cross-stitch made by himself when a child but five years of age. He is deft with his fingers, and, as the saying is, "can turn his hand to anything." May it not be that the manipulation then acquired still serves him?

Another man tells laughingly how, when a boy at college, he would tie up the hole, in his socks with a piece of string, and then hammer the hard lump flat with a stone. He could as easily make a gown as darn a stocking. Tales such as this fill motherly souls with intense pity for the poor fellow so powerless to take care of his clothing, and so far from any woman-helper. If possible, teach your boy enough of the rudiments of plain sewing to help him in an emergency, so that he can put on a button, or stitch up a rip, when absent from you.

As many men as women have a natural bias for cookery, and there are husbands not a few who insist on making all the salad eaten on their tables.

One branch of work in which boys are sinfully deficient is "putting things to rights." The floor of your son's room may be littered with books, papers, cravats, soiled collars and cuffs, but he never thinks it his duty to pick them up and to keep his possessions in order. About one man in a thousand is an exception to this rule, and thrice blessed is she who weds him. It goes without saying in the household that by some occult principle of natural adaptation, there is always a "time" for a man to scatter abroad and for a woman to gather together. Mother or sister attends to "the boy's things." Why has the boy any more than the girl the right to leave his hat on the parlor table, his gloves on the mantel, his coat on the newel-post, and his over-shoes in the middle of the floor? They are left there, and there they remain until some long-suffering woman puts them away. From hut to palace, and through uncounted generations, by oral and written enactment, as well as by tacit consent, whatever other innovations are made, the custom holds that man can upset without fault, and his nearest of feminine kin is blamable if she do not "pick up after him."

Teach your son that it is his business to keep his own room in order, and that there is no more reason why his sister should follow him up, replacing what he has disarranged, than that he should perform the same office for her. Inculcate in him habits of neatness. In acquiring an "eye" for the disorder he has caused, and deftness in rectifying it, he is taking lessons in tender consideration and growing in intelligent sympathy for mother, sister and the wife who-is-to-be.

CHAPTER XX

CHILDREN AS BURDEN-BEARERS

Those of us who are mothers would do well to read carefully and ponder deeply St. Paul's assertion that when he was a child he spoke as a child, and felt as a child, and thought as a child; and that when he was a man, and not until then, he put away childish things.

Can the same be said of the child of to-day?

In this "bit of talk," I want to enter my protest against thrusting upon children the care-taking thought that should not be theirs for years to come. When the responsibility that is inseparable from every life bears heavily upon us, we sigh for the carefree days of childhood, but we do not hesitate to inflict upon our babies the complaints and moans which teach them, all too soon, that life is a hard school for us. A child must either grieve with us or become so inured to our plaints that he pays no attention to them. In the latter case he may be hard-hearted but he is certainly happier than if he were exquisitely sensitive.

"What a pretty suit of clothes you have!" said I to a four-year-old boy.

The momentary expression of pride gave way to one

of anxiety.

"Yes; but mamma says when these wear out she does not know how papa will ever buy me any more clothes. I am a great expense! Oh!" with a long-drawn sigh of wretchedness, "isn't it *awful* to be poor?"

The poverty-stricken father was at this time managing to dress himself, wife and baby on an income of four thousand dollars per annum. In her desire to make her child take proper care of his clothes, the mother had struck terror to the little fellow's heart. Such childish terror is genuine, and yet hard to express. The self-control of childhood is far greater than the average father or mother appreciates. Some children seem to have an actual dread of communicating their fears and fancies to other people.

A friend tells me that when she was but six years old she heard her father say impatiently, as his wife handed him a bill:

"I can't pay this! At the rate at which bills come in nowadays, I soon will not have a cent left in the world. It is enough to bankrupt a man!"

At bedtime that night the little daughter asked her mother, with the indifferent air children so soon learn to assume:

"Mamma, what becomes of people when all their money is gone, and they can't pay their bills?"

"Sometimes, dear," answered the unsuspicious mother, "their houses and belongings are sold to pay their bills."

"And when people have no house, and no money, and nothing left, where do they go? Do they starve to death?"

"They generally go to the poorhouse, my daughter."

"Oh, mamma!" quavered the little voice, "don't you think that is dreadful?"

"Very dreadful, darling! Now go to sleep."

To sleep! How could she, with the grim doors of the home for the county paupers yawning blackly to receive her? All through the night was the horror upon her, and to this day she remembers the sickening thrill that swept over her while playing with a little friend, when the thought occurred:

"If this girl's mother knew that we were going to the poorhouse, she would not let her play with me."

Little by little the impression wore off, aided in the dissipation by the sight of numerous rolls of bills which papa occasionally drew from his pocket. But not once in all that time did the child relax the strict guard set upon her lips, and sob out her fear to her mother. She does not now know why she did not do it, except that she could not.

An otherwise judicious father talks over all his business difficulties with his seven-year-old son. The grown man does not know what a strain the anxiety and uncertainty of his father's ventures are to the embryo financier. Not long ago the father announced to him:

"Well, Harold, that man I was telling you of has failed—lost his money—and one thousand dollars of mine have gone with it."

The boy's white, set face would have alarmed a more observant man.

"Oh, papa! what shall we do!"

"Get along somehow, my boy!" was the unsatisfactory answer.

Then, as the boy sadly and slowly left the room, the man to whom one thousand dollars were no more than one dime to this anxious child, explained, laughingly, to a friend, that "that little fellow was really wonderful; he understood business, and was as much interested in it as a man of forty could be."

We fathers and mothers have no right to make our children old before their time. Each age has its own trials, which are as great as any one person should bear. We know that the troubles that come to our babies are only baby troubles, but they are as large to them as our griefs are to us. A promised drive, which does not "materialize," proves as great a disappointment to your tiny girl as the unfulfilled promise of a week in the country would to you, her sensible mother. Of course our children must learn to bear their trials. My plea is that they may not be forced to bear our anxieties also. If a thing is an annoyance to you, it will be an agony to your little child, who has not a tenth of your experience, philosophy and knowledge of life.

There is something cowardly and weak in the man or woman who has so little self-control that he or she must press a child's tender shoulders into service in bearing burdens. Teach your children to be careful, teach them prudence and economy, but let them be taught as children.

The forcing of a child's sympathies sometimes produces a hardening effect, as in the case of a small boy whose mother was one of the sickly-sentimental sort. She had drawn too often upon her child's sensibilities.

"Charlie," she said, plaintively, to her youngest boy, "what would you do if poor mamma were to get very sick?"

"Send for the doctor."

"But, Charlie, suppose poor, dear mamma should die! Then, what would you do?"

"I'd go to the funeral!" was the cheerful response.

To my mind this mother had the son ordained for her from the beginning of the world.

Many boys are all love and sympathy for their mothers. Mamma appeals to all that is tender and chivalrous in the nature of the man that is to be. The maternal tenderness ought to be too strong to impose upon this sacred feeling.

Perhaps one of the prettiest of Bunner's "Airs from Arcady" is that entitled, "In School Hours," in which he thus describes the woe of the thirteen-year-old girl when she receives the cruel letter from the boy of her admiration. The poet tells us this sorrow "were tragic at thirty," and asks, "Why is it trivial at thirteen!"

"Trivial! what shall eclipse
The pain of our childish woes?
The rose-bud pales its lips
When a very small zephyr blows.
You smile, O Dian bland,
If Endymion's glance is cold:
But Despair seems close at hand
To that hapless thirteen-year old!"

CHAPTER XXI

OUR YOUNG PERSON

I well remember a girl's tearful appeal to me when she was stigmatized and reproved for her "giddy youth!" "It is not my fault that I was born young! And I am not responsible for the fact that I entered upon existence seventeen, instead of seventy, years ago. At all events, it was not a sin even if I was guilty of such a folly!"

Perhaps we older people are too prone to forget that youth is not a sin to be condemned, or even a folly to be sneered at. "Wad some power the giftie gie us" to remember that we were not always cool-headed, clear-seeing and middle-aged! Trouble and responsibility come so soon to all, that we err in forcing young heads to bow, and strong shoulders to bend, beneath a load which should not be laid upon them for many years. As we advance in age, our weaknesses and temptations change, and no longer take the form of heedlessness, intolerance, extravagance, and most trying of all to the critical and dignified observer,—freshness.

We may describe this last-named quality somewhat after the fashion of the little boy who defined salt as "What makes potatoes taste bad when they don't put any on 'em!"

So "freshness" is that which makes youth delightful by

its absence.

Unfortunately, it is almost inseparable from this period, and while there are girls, and even boys, in whom the offending quality is nearly, if not entirely, lacking, they are almost as the red herring of the wood, and the strawberry of the sea, in nursery rhyme.

Freshness takes many and varied forms, the most common being that of self-conceit and the desire to appear original and eccentric in feelings, moods, likes and dislikes. Like the fellows of the club of which Bertie, in "The Henrietta," was an illustrious member, the average boy winks, nods, looks wise and "makes the other fellows think that he is a Harry of a fellow,—but he isn't!"

The desire to be considered worldly-wise—"tough"—is rampant in the masculine mind between the ages of fifteen and twenty. The boy who has been to a strict preparatory boarding-school and is just entering upon his college course, whose theatre-goings have been limited to the "shows" to which his father has given him tickets, or to which he has escorted his mother or sisters, and whose wildest dissipations have consisted in a surreptitious cigarette and glass of beer, neither of which he enjoyed, but both of which he pretended to revel in for the sake of being "mannish,"—will talk knowingly of "the latest soubrette," "a jolly little ballet-dancer," "the wicked ways of this world," and "the dens of iniquity in our large cities." Dickens tells us that "when Mr. Feeder spoke of the dark mysteries of London, and told Mr. Toots that he was going to observe it himself closely in all its ramifications in the approaching holidays, and for that purpose had made arrangements to board with two old maiden aunts at Peckham, Paul regarded him as if he were the hero of some book of travel or wild adventure, and was almost afraid of such a slashing person."

Why it is considered manly to be "tough" is one of the unsolved mysteries of the boyish mind. Any uneducated, weak fool can go wrong. It takes a man to be strong enough to keep himself pure and good.

Another "fresh" characteristic of this age is the pretence of doubt. A fellow under twenty-one is likely to have doubts, to find articles in the creed of his church "to which he cannot agree. That kind of thing is well enough for women and children, but for a man of the world,"—and then follows an expressive pause, accompanied by a shrug of the shoulders and lift of the brows.

With a girl this trying age is often given over to sentimental musings and blues. She is convinced that nobody under-stands her, her mother least of all, that she is too sensitive for this harsh world, that she will never receive the love and consideration due her. Cynicism becomes her main charac-teristic, and she bitterly sneers at friendship and gratitude, declaring that true, disinterested affection exists only in the imagination. Is it any wonder that mothers sometimes become discouraged? Poor mothers! whose combined comfort and distress is the knowledge that the time is fast approaching when their boys and girls will blush for shame at the remembrance of their "salad days, when they were green in judgment."

Parents have need of vast patience, and let them, before uttering condemnation, carefully consider if they themselves are not a little to blame for the state of their children's minds; if over-indulgence and unwise consideration have not had much to do with the trouble. One excellent woman has made of her son an insufferable boor by constantly deferring to him, no matter in what company, and by allowing him to see that she considers his very ordinary intellect far above the average. In a parlor full of educated men and women she went out of her way to tell what remarkable views "Charlie" had upon certain religious subjects, and, after attracting the attention of the assembled company, called upon "Charlie" to give vent to his sentiments that all present might observe how original they were. Whereupon the hulk of a son, consequential and patronizing, discoursed bunglingly, and at length, on his opinions and beliefs, until he was inflated to speechlessness by conceit, and his hearers disgusted into responsive silence.

If your girl is clever, do not tell her so, or repeat to others in her presence her bright observations. But, on the other hand, do not snub her, or allow her to feel that her intellect is of an inferior order. The best way to make a fool of the Young Person is to tell him that he is a fool. Stimulate your child by all the love and appreciation at your command, but let it be intelligent appreciation, not blind admiration or prejudiced disapproval. Do you recollect how you felt and dreamed and gushed when you were a girl, the pages of sentimental twaddle (as you now call it) which you confided to the diary which you burned in disgust at twenty-one? Do you remember how genuine your distresses then seemed? You can smile at the girl you once were, but still you find it in your heart to pity her, poor, silly child, foolishly sobbing late into the night over some broken friendship or imaginary heart-trouble. Perhaps she had no mother to whom to go, or perhaps her mother "did not understand." See that you do not make the same mistake, but, while you recognize the folly of the trouble, think of the heartache back of it all. When your girl was a tiny child, you petted and comforted her as she wailed over her broken dolly. Was that grief so much more sensible than this, or do you love her less now? When your four-year-old boy came to you with his stories of what he would do when he was "a great big man," you drew him close to you and encouraged him to "talk it all out." Now, when he is a head taller than you, and tells you of his hopes and aspirations, you sigh that "boys are so fresh and visionary!"

It is not necessary to condone or to condemn all. What would you say to the gardener who let your choice young vines run in straggling lines all over the ground and in all directions,—or who ruthlessly cut off all the stalks within an inch of the roots? Young people need training, encouragement and urging in some directions, repression and pruning in others. Above all, they need tender forbearance.

Another trying feature of the Young Person is his wholesale intolerance of everything and everybody. Only himself and perhaps one or two of his own friends escape his censure. These being covered with the mantle of his approbation, are beyond criticism. This habit of uncharitableness is such an odious one that our boy or girl should avoid it carefully.

If you would acquire the custom of saying no evil, it is advisable to guard against thinking it. Difficult as it may seem, it is quite possible to put such a guard upon the mind as to accustom it to look on the best side of persons and things. Nobody is wholly bad, or, at least, few people are so entirely given over to disagreeable traits as the Young Person would lead us to think. Only a few days ago a young man was speaking in my presence of another fellow, who was, as far as I know, a respectable, well-bred boy.

"Oh!" said the Young Person, when his name was mentioned, "he is no good."

"Why not?" queried I. "Is he bad?"

"He is too much of a fool to be bad."

"Is he such a fool? I thought he was considered rather bright?"

"Well, he thinks himself awfully bright. He is a regular donkey."

"Are his manners disagreeable?"

"No-o-o, I don't know that they are. In fact, I believe he prides himself on the reputation he has acquired for gentlemanliness."

"Then, what is so disagreeable about him?"

"Perhaps," dryly suggested the father of the Young Person, "he is not particularly fond of you, and that it why you disapprove of him."

"No, sir!" was the indignant rejoinder, "that is not it. To be sure, he never troubles himself to pay me any marked attention. Nor do I care to have him do so. He is a low fellow."

Deny it as he might, the reason my young friend disliked the "low fellow" was because the tiny thorn of neglect had wounded his vanity and pricked and rankled into a fester. This is human nature, but as we advance in years, we appreciate that people may be really excellent in many respects, and yet have no great fondness for us. Youth still has much to learn.

Ten girls whom I know formed a society for the repression of unkind criticism. The members pledged themselves to try, as far as in them lay, to speak kindly of people when it was possible for them to do so, and when impossible to say nothing. At first it was hard, for self-conceit would intrude, and it is hard for one girl to praise another who dislikes her. Little by little the tiny seed of effort grew into a habit of kindly speech.

What volumes it argues for a woman's gentle ladyhood and Christianity when it can truthfully be said of her, "She never speaks uncharitably of anybody!"

Let us older people set an example of tolerance and charitable speech. Too often our children are but reproductions, perhaps somewhat highly colored, of ourselves, our virtues, and our faults. And this is especially true of the mothers. John Jarndyce gives us a word of encouragement when he says—

"I think it must somewhere be written that the virtues of the mothers shall occasionally be visited upon the children, as well as the sins of the father."

Such being the case, let us children of a larger growth show such tact, unselfishness and tender charity, that our children, seeing these virtues, may copy them, and thereby aid in removing the disagreeable traits of, at least, our Young Persons.

CHAPTER XXII

OUR BOY

The following is a *bona fide* letter. It is written in such genuine earnest, and so clearly voices the sentiments of many young men of the present day, that I am glad to have an opportunity to answer it.

1. Why should I, a fast-growing, hard-working youth of eighteen, who go every morning, four miles by street-car, to my office, and the same back at night, often so weary and faint as to be hardly able to sit, not to say stand, be obliged to give up my seat to any flighty, flashy girl who has come down-town to shop, or frolic, or do nothing? Isn't she as able to "swing corners" holding on to a strap as I? and to hold her own perpendicular in the aisle?

2. Why isn't it as rude for her and her companions to giggle and whisper and stare, the objects of amusement being her fellow-passengers, as it would be for me and my fellows? Yet we would be "roughs"—and she and her crew must be "treated with the deference due the gentler sex." And why am I a boor if I do not give her my seat, while she is considered a lady if she takes it without thanking me?

3. Are girls, take them as a rule, as well-bred as boys?

Judging by appearances, it would seem that many men share in the feeling expressed in your first query. I am not a "flighty, flashy girl," but I crossed the city the other night in a horse-car in which there were twenty men and two women—one of them being myself. I stood, while the score of men sat and lounged comfortably behind their news-papers. They were tired after a hard day's work, and would have been wearied still more by standing. A well woman was worn out and a delicate woman would have been made ill, by this exertion.

My dear boy! let me ask you one question. Why should you, no matter how tired you are, spring eagerly forward to prevent your sister from lifting a piece of furniture, or carrying a trunk upstairs? Why not let her do it? I can imagine your look of indignant surprise. "Why? because she is a woman! It would nearly kill her!" Exactly so; but you will swing the burden on your broad, strong shoulders, bear it to its destination, and the next minute run lightly down-stairs,—perhaps, as you would say, "a little winded," but not one whit strained in nerve or muscle.

There lies the difference. The good Lord who made us women had His own excellent reason for making us physically weaker than men. Perhaps because, had we their strength, we would be too ambitious. However that may be, men, as the stronger sex, should help us in our weakness. Standing in the horse-car that is jostling over a rough track, holding on with up-stretched arm to a strap and "swinging corners" during a two-mile ride, would do more harm to a girl of your own age than you would suffer were you to stand while making a twenty-mile trip. For humanity's sake, then, if your gallantry does not prompt you to make sacrifice, do not allow any woman, old or young, to "hold her perpendicular in the aisle" when you can offer her a seat and while you have a pair of capable legs upon which to depend for support.

A true gentleman is always unselfish, be he old or young, rested or weary; and such being the case, the foreign day-laborer, in blue blouse and hob-nailed boots, who rises and gives a lady his place in car or omnibus, is the superior of the several-times-a-millionaire, in finest broadcloth, spotless linen, patent leathers and silk hat, who sits still, taking refuge behind his newspaper, in which he is seemingly so deeply absorbed as to be blind to the fact that a woman, old enough to be his mother, stands near him. With one gentlemanliness is instinctive, with the other it is, like his largest diamond stud, worn for show, and even then is a little "off color." I hope it is hardly necessary to remind you that true courtesy does not stay to distinguish between a rich or a poor woman, or to notice whether she is a pretty young girl, fashionably attired, or a decrepit laundress taking home the week's wash. She is a woman! That should be sufficient to arouse your manliness.

This is the truthful reply to query No. 1. Not a pleasant answer perhaps, but an honest one. To make the advice more palatable, take it with a plentiful seasoning of gratitude for the gift of physical strength which makes you a man.

And now for No. 2. Here you are right, and your suggestion has had my serious consideration. Possibly, thoughtlessness may account for the foolish "whispering and giggling" you mention, but stares and amused comments upon fellow-passengers are nothing less than acts of rudeness, be they perpetrated by boy or girl. But two wrongs never yet made a right, and because a girl is discourteous is no reason why you should put yourself on the same footing with her, and fail to observe towards her "the deference due" all women. If you are in a car with a profane drunkard, you do not copy his actions, or, if obliged to address him, adopt his style of language.

The glaring defect in the manners and voice of the American girl is that she is "loud." German Gretchen or Irish Bridget is more likely to speak softly in public than her rich young mistress. It is often a shock to the observer when sweet sixteen seated opposite him in the horse-car, begins conversation with her companion. Her face is gentle, her whole mien refined,—but, her voice! She talks loudly and laughs constantly. One beautiful woman whom I have met,—wealthy and well-educated, always reminds me of a peacock. You doubtless have seen and heard peafowls often enough to understand the comparison. The graceful motion and gorgeous plumage demand our admiration, until the creature, becoming accustomed to our presence, raises his voice in a piercing call, something between a hoot and a shriek, which causes us to cover our ears. After such an experience, we turn with relief to the sober hens who are contented to cluck peacefully through life, reserving their cackling until they have done something of which to boast, and wish to inform us that the egg they have laid is at our disposal.

As a rule the girl who is *prononcee* in a public conveyance is not well-bred, and she who laughs loudly and talks noisily, meanwhile passing comments on those persons who are so unfortunate as to be her traveling companions, has no claim to the much-abused title of "lady." But you can hardly compare your manners and those of your friends with the deportment of low-born, ill-bred girls. I fancy that you would find that everyone would pronounce sentence as severe upon them as upon you, were your actions the same.

I have been amazed before this at what I have been told, and at what I have myself noticed, of the failure of women to thank men who rise and offer them seats.

It would seem incredible that any person should so far neglect all semblance of civility as to accept a place thus offered as a matter of course. It is a kindness on the part of a man, and should always be met by some acknowledgment. If, when you rise, and lifting your hat, resign your place to a woman, and she, without a word, accepts it as her due, your only consolation will be to fall back on the comforting thought that you have behaved like a gentleman, and that any discourtesy of hers cannot detract from the merit of your action. You did not do it for the thanks you might receive, but because it is right. It is not pessimistic to assert that all through life, we are working on this principle—not that we may receive the credit for what we do, but doing good for the good's sake. Do not be so rash as to say bitterly—"So much for sacrificing my own comfort!" "Catch me giving a woman my seat again!" and those other foolish, because angry, things which a vexed boy is tempted to say under such circumstances. Continue in the good way, hoping that "next time" you may have the pleasure of doing a favor to a lady who has the breeding to appreciate and be grateful for an act of courtesy.

Your third question is one difficult to answer. Are girls as well bred as boys—Yes—and no! Their training lies along different lines. A few days ago I was talking with a young man who had a grievance. A girl of his acquaintance had, the night before, been at a reception which he had also attended. Feeling a little weary she retired to a comfortable corner of the room, and sat there during the entire evening. She "did not feel like dancing," and told her hostess "she would rather sit still." My young friend had a severe headache, but, although suffering, his appreciation of *les convenances* would not allow him to sit down in a secluded niche for fifteen minutes, during the entire evening. His "grievance" was that had he done this he would have been voted a boor, while the girl's action was condoned by hostess and guests. One thing must always be considered—namely, that a woman's part is, in many points of etiquette, passive. It is the man who takes the initiative, and who is

Marion Harland

made such a prominent figure that all eyes are drawn to him. Have you ever noticed it? Man proposes, woman accepts. Man stands, woman remains seated. Man lifts his hat, woman merely bows. Man acts as escort, woman as the escorted. So, when a man is careless or thoughtless, it is all the more evident. For this reason, begin as a boy, to observe all the small, sweet courtesies of life. I often wish there were any one point in which a woman could show her genuine ladyhood as a man displays his gentlehood by the management of his hat,—raising it entirely from the head on meeting a woman, lifting it when the lady with whom he is walking bows to an acquaintance, or when his man-companion meets a friend, baring his head on meeting, parting from, or kissing mother, sister or wife. These, with other points, such as rising when a woman enters the room, and remaining standing until she is seated, giving her the precedence in passing in or out of a door, and picking up the handkerchief or glove she lets fall—are sure indices of the gentleman, or, by their absence, mark the boor.

But our girl should not think that she can afford to overlook the acts of tactful courtesy which are her duty as well as her brother's. Prominent among these she should place the deference due those who are older than herself. Her temptation is often to exercise a patronizing toleration toward her elders, and, while she is not actually disrespectful, she still has the air of a very superior young being holding converse with a person who has the advantage merely in the accident of years. Did she realize how ridiculous these very youthful, foolish manners are, she would blush for herself. She will—when she has attained the age of discretion.

Another of our girls' mistakes is that of imagining that brusqueness and pertness are wit. There is no other error more common with girls from fifteen to eighteen; they generally choose a boy as the butt of their sarcastic remarks—and, to their shame be it said, they frequently select a lad who is too courteous to retort in kind.

But these faults in boy and girl alike are evidences of a "freshness" which wears off as the years roll on, as the green husk, when touched by the frost, falls away, leaving exposed the glossy brown shell enclosing the ripe, sweet kernel of the nut.

If this answer to your letter reads like a sermon, pardon one who is interested in young people, and who, well remembering when she was young herself, would fain hold out a helping hand to those who are stumbling on in the path she trod in years gone by.

Marion Harland

CHAPTER XXIII

THAT SPOILED CHILD

I was the other day one of many passengers in a railroad train in which a small girl of four or five years of age was making a journey, accompanied by her mother and an aunt. The child was beautiful, with a mass of golden curls. Her velvet coat and the felt hat trimmed elaborately with ostrich plumes were faultless in their style; her behavior would compare unfavorably with the manners of a young Comanche Indian. She insisted upon standing in the centre of the aisle, where she effectually blocked all passage, and, as the train was going rapidly, ran a great risk of being thrown violently against the seats. When remonstrated with by her guardians, she slapped her aunt full in the face, pulled herself free from her mother's restraining grasp, and, in a frenzy of rage, threw herself down right across the aisle. There she lay for a full half hour. When her mother would have raised her to her feet she uttered shriek after shriek, until her fellow-travelers' ears rang. After this triumph of young America over the rule and command of tyrannizing mamma, the innocent babe was allowed to remain prostrate in her chosen resting-place, while brakemen, conductor and passengers stepped gingerly over the recumbent form. She varied the monotony of the situation by occasional wrathful kicks in the direction of her mother or at some would-be passer-by.

"It is best to let sleeping dogs lie," sighed the mother of this prodigy to her sister. "When she gets one of these attacks (and she has them quite often) I just leave her alone until she becomes ashamed of it. She can't bear to be crossed in anything."

When I stepped from the train at my destination the humiliation for which her attendants longed was still a stranger to the willful child.

Trouble-fearing persons have a belief to the effect that it is, in the long run, easier to let a child have his own sweet way until he has attained the age of discretion,—say at fourteen or fifteen years,—when his innate sense of propriety will convince him of the error of his ways. Such a theorist was a dear old gentleman who, many years ago, remonstrated with me upon the pains and time I spent in training my first born. The children of this aged saint had been reared according to the old-fashioned notion, but when they had babies of their own they departed from it, and the rising generation had full and free sway. Their grandparent, albeit frequently the victim of their pranks, loved them dearly. He now assured me that—

"While they are regular little barbarians, my dear, still they have all that freedom and wild liberty which should accompany childhood. They eat when and what they please, go to bed when they feel like it, rise early or late as the whim seizes them, and know no prescribed rules for diet and deportment. But they come of good stock and will turn out all right."

They did come of good, honest parents, and this may have been what saved their moral, while their physical being has suffered from the course pursued during their infancy and early youth. There were six children; now there are four. One died when a mere baby from cold contracted from running about the house in winter weather in her bare feet. She was so fond of doing this that her mother could not bear to put shoes and stockings on the dear little tot. The other, a sweet, affectionate boy, suffered at regular intervals during the fifteen years of his life from acute indigestion. Directly after one of these attacks, he, as was his habit, followed the cravings of an undisciplined appetite, and attended, late at night, a pea-nut-and-candy supper, almost immediately after which he was taken violently ill and died in three days. The four remaining children do not, all told, possess enough constitution to make one strong man. They are all delicate and constant sufferers.

In this case judicious care might have averted the above-mentioned evils. Would the game have been worth the candle?

This is a question which parents cannot afford to disregard. It is expedient for them to consider seriously whether or not the stock on both sides of the family, of which their children come, is so good as to warrant neglect or to justify over-indulgence.

Our mother-tongue does not offer us a phrase by which we may express what we mean by *l'enfant terrible*. But our father-land produces many living examples which may serve as translations of the French words. Such an one was the small boy who, while eagerly devouring grapes, threw the skins, one after another, into the lap of my new light silk gown. His mother entered a smilingly gentle protest in the form of—

"Oh, Frankie dear! do you think it is pretty to do that?" to which he paid as much attention as to my look of distress. The reader who believes in "lending a hand" in righting the minor evils of society must have more temerity and a larger share of what the boy of the period denominates "nerve" than I possess, if she interferes with a child while in the presence of the mother. It is as unsafe as the proverbial act of inserting the digits between the bark and the tree. It is, moreover, a liberty which I should never permit the dearest friend to take. In fact, so strong is my feeling on this subject, that I should have allowed "Frankie dear" to make a fruit-plate and finger-bowl of the shimmering folds of my gown rather than utter a feeble objection before his doting mamma.

The practice of spoiling a child is unjust to the little one and to the parent. The latter suffers tenfold more than if she, day by day, inculcated the line-upon-line, protest-upon-protest system. That she does not do this is sometimes due to mistaken kindness, but oftener to self-indulgence or dread of disagreeable scenes, that brings a harvest of misery as surely as he who sows the wind will reap the whirlwind.

A spoiled child is an undutiful child. This must be true. The constant humoring and considering of one's whims will, in course of time, produce a stunted, warped and essentially selfish character, that considers the claims of gratitude and affection as *nil* compared with the furtherance of personal aims and desires. Never having learned self-control or obedience, parents and their timid remonstrances must go to the wall before the passions or longings which these same parents in days gone by have fostered. "Only mother" or "nobody but father" are phrases that are so frequent as to become habitual, while the "you yourself used to let me do this or that" is the burden of many an excuse for misdemeanors. And after all the years of parental indulgence, what is your reward? The spring is gone from your own being, while your children will not let you live your life over again in theirs.

We all recall AEsop's fable of the young man about to be executed, who begged on the scaffold for a last word with his mother, and when the wish was granted, stooped to her and bit off the tip of her ear, that the pain and disfigurement might serve as a constant reminder of the hatred he felt for the over-indulgence and lack of discipline which had brought him to this shameful death. The hurt which the mother's heart feels at the thought of causing her child's downfall is pain too great to be endured.

The letting-alone principle is a short-sighted one. Even in infancy a spoiled child may make such a nuisance of himself as to produce a disagreeable impression upon all who know him,—an impression which it takes many years of model behavior to eradicate. It is actual cruelty to throw upon the child the work the parent should have performed. It is easy to train the growing plant, but after the bark is tough and the fibre strong it is a terrible strain upon grain and vitality to bend it in a direction to which it is unaccustomed.

Much of the insubordination to be found in the children of the present day is due to the growing habit of entrusting the little ones to servants whose own wills and tempers are uncontrolled and untrained. A child knows that his nurse has no right to insist upon obedience, and he takes advantage of the knowledge until he is a small tyrant who is conscious of no law beyond that of his own inclinations.

The prime rule in the training of children should be implicit obedience. The child is happier for knowing that when a command or prohibition is stated there is no appeal from the sentence, and that coaxing avails naught. Uncertainty is as trying to small men and women as to us who are more advanced in the school of life.

So much depends upon this great principle of obedience, that it is marvelous that parents ever disregard it. I have known in my own experience three cases in which it was impossible to make a child take medicine, and death has followed in consequence. One of the most painful recollections I have is of seeing a child six years old forced to swallow a febrifuge that was not unpalatable in itself. The mother, father, and nurse held the struggling boy, while the physician pried open the set teeth and poured the liquid down his throat. Under these circumstances it is probable that the remedy proved worse than the disease.

I have not space to do more than touch upon the great influence of early training on the future life. All my days I have been thankful for the gentle but firm hand that, as a child, taught me moral courage, self-denial and submission. The temptations of life have been more easily resisted, the trials more lightly borne, because of the years in which I was in training for the race set before me. We do not want to enter our children on the course as unbroken, "soft" and wild colts, whose spirits must be crushed before they will submit to the work assigned them. They may be young, yet strong; spirited, yet gentle; patient, yet resolute.

Marion Harland

CHAPTER XXIV

GETTING ALONG IN YEARS

"Does your husband think a full beard becoming to him?" asked I of a young wife.

Her twenty-three-year-old lord, whose good-looking face had been adorned and made positively handsome by a sweeping brown moustache, had, since our last meeting, "raised" an uneven crop of reddish whiskers that shortened a face somewhat too round, and altogether vulgarized what had been refined.

"No, indeed! He knows, as I do, that it disfigures him. It is a business necessity to which he sacrificed vanity. The appearance of maturity carries weight in the commercial world. His beard adds ten years to his real age."

Being in an audience collected to hear an eminent clergyman last summer, I heard an astonished gasp behind me, as the orator arose:

"Why he has shaved off his beard! How like a round oily man of God he looks!"

"True," said another, "but fifteen years younger. He is getting along in years, you see, and wants to hide the fact."

The last speaker sat opposite to me at the hotel table that day, and in discussing the leader of the morning service, repeated the phrase that had jarred upon my ear.

"It is fatal to a clergyman's popularity and to a woman's hopes to be suspected of getting along in years."

I told the story of my bearded youth and asked:

"Where then is the safe ground? When is it altogether reputable for one to declare his real age?"

"Oh, anywhere from thirty to forty-five! Before and after that term life can hardly be said to be worth the living."

I smiled, as the rattler meant I should. But the words have stayed by me, the more persistently that observation bears me out in the suspicion that the merry speaker only uttered the thought of many others.

"The years of man's life are three-score-and-ten," says the Word of Him who made man and knew what was in man. The wearer of a body that, with tolerably good treatment ought to last for seventy years, must then, according to popular judgment, spend nearly half of that time in learning how to play his part in the world, barely a fifth in carrying out God's designs in and for him, and then remain for a quarter of a century a cumberer of the home and earth. Such waste of strength, time and accumulated capital would be cried out upon as wretched mismanagement were the scheme of human devising.

The French proverb that "a woman" (and presumably a man) "is just as old as she chooses to be," comes so much nearer what I believe was our Creator's wise and merciful purpose in giving us life, that I turn thankfully and hopefully to this side of the subject.

Marion Harland

The best way to avoid growing old is not to be afraid of getting along in years. To come down to "hard pan"— whence originates this unwholesome dread of ripeness and maturity? It surely is not a fear of death that makes us blanch and shrink back at the oft-recurring mile-stones in the journey of life that brings all of us nearer the goal towards which we are bound.

I once heard a young woman say, seriously:

"I hope that when I am forty-five, I may quietly die. I do not dread death, but I do shudder at the idea of being laid on the shelf."

I do not mean to be severe when I assert that, nine times out of ten, it is the victim's own fault that she is pushed out of the way, or, as our slangy youth of to-day put it, "is not in it." It is your business and mine to *be* in it, heart, soul, and body, and to keep our places there by every effort in our power. A fear of that which is high, or mental or physical inertia, or, to be less euphemistic and more exact, laziness— should not deter us. This object is not to be accomplished by adopting juvenile dress and kittenish ways. We should beautify old age, not accentuate it by artificial means. When your roadster, advanced in years and woefully stiff in the joints, makes a lame attempt to imitate a gamboling colt, and feebly elevates his hind legs, and pretends to shy at a piece of paper in the road, you smile with contemptuous amusement and say:

"The old fool is in his dotage!"

But if he keeps on steadily to his work, doing the best he can, your comment is sure to be somewhat after this fashion:

"This is truly a wonderful horse! He is just as good as on the day I bought him, fifteen years ago!"

Let us determine to face the situation, when it is necessary, calmly and sensibly. For, unlike the aforesaid horse, we do not expect to be knocked on the head with a club, or quietly chloroformed out of existence at a stated period. We would do well to follow our optimistic principles, and look at the many benefits which, in the words of the old catechism, "do accompany and flow from" this state. If you have lived well, fifty is better than thirty, as the sun-and-frost-kissed (not bitten) Catawba grape is better than the tiny green sphere of June, and as maturity is nearer perfection than crude youth. The tedious routine of the life-school, the hours spent in acquiring knowledge for which you had no immediate use, are past. The wisdom that must come with time and experience is yours.

Another of the great advantages in being near the top of the mountain is that you can speak from superior knowledge words of comfort and encouragement to those beneath you, who are still toiling over the path you have trod. Such help from you who have "been there," and have now successfully passed the most trying places, will do more to keep up others' hearts than many sermons preached by one who knows it all only in theory.

Since old age is inevitable, do not let us try to pretend that it is not, and let us never act as if there were any hope of shunning it. On the other hand, neither should we wish that it were possible for us to evade it. It is just as much of a God-ordained period as youth, and we ought to grow old in the manner in which God meant we should. He meant us to keep heart and soul young by constant occupation and by unselfish interest in the affairs of others.

I know one woman, past the fifties, who is, the young people declare, "much more fun than any girl." Their enjoyments are hers, and she laughs as heartily over their fun, sympathizes as sincerely in their disappointments, as if she were thirty years younger than she is. In fact, her sympathy is more genuine, for her age puts her completely beyond the faintest suspicion of rivalry, and it is easier to tell of one's defeats and triumphs when the listener is too far along in years to be jealous or envious.

It should not be necessary for us to call courage into use to reconcile us to our lost youth. Plain common sense is all that is requisite. We have gained much on life in the past century. As science has taught us how to ward off death, so has it instructed us in the art of preserving youth far beyond middle age. Over my fireplace hangs a portrait of my grandmother, one of the loveliest women of her time.

She died at the age of fifty, and in it she wears a mob-cap and an old woman's gown. For years before her death, she felt that she belonged to the past generation, did not join in the younger people's occupations, and claimed her place in the chimney-corner. In her day the "dead-line" in a man's life was drawn at fifty. Now we know that to be out of all reason. If the years of a man's life are three-score-and-ten let us determine to move the dead-line on to seventy, and claim that we are not old until we have reached that point. And if, by reason of strength we can hold on to four-score, let us push it on the ten years farther, and, taking courage, thank God for this new lease of life.

We do not belong to the past generation, but to the acting, working, living present. Our juniors are the rising generation, and no one belongs to the past except those who have laid aside the burden of life—light to some, wearisome to others—forever. They are the only ones who have any excuse for stepping out of the ranks. They have done so by their Captain's order. Let us, who remain, stand bravely in our places, that we may be present or accounted for when the roll-call containing our names is read.

Marion Harland

CHAPTER XXV

TRUTH-TELLING

"Conformity to fact or reality. Exact accordance with that which is, has been, or shall be."

I looked up Webster's definition of Truth yesterday, after overhearing a conversation between two girls in the horse-car. They spoke so loudly that not to hear would have been an impossibility. My attention was first attracted to them by the name of a friend.

"Did you know of Mr. B.'s illness?" asked the younger and more pronounced colloquist.

"Yes," responded the other; "I know he has had pneumonia, but I understand that he is now convalescent."

"Oh, then, you haven't heard the latest!"

The discovery of her companion's ignorance acted upon the girl like magic. She became vivacious, and beamed with the glow of satisfaction kindled by the privilege of being the first to relate a morsel of news.

"Well, my dear! Mamma and I were calling there, and while I was talking to Miss B., I heard Mrs. B. tell my mother this awful thing. You know Mr. B.'s sister is a trained nurse (I never did believe in trained nurses!) and when he was taken so ill they sent for her to come and take care of him. She got along tolerably well until a few days ago when the doctor prescribed quinine for Mr. B. By mistake, she gave him ten grains of morphine."

"What!"

"Yes, my dear, she did! It seems like an immense quantity, but, as I wanted to be accurate (I always say that accuracy is a Christian duty), I asked Miss B. how many grains her father took, and she said 'Ten!' Well! the poor victim slept thirty hours, and they were so frightened that they sent for the doctor. He said that, fortunately, no harm was done, but that it was an unpardonable piece of carelessness. They discharged the nurse forthwith. She ought to have been arrested and punished,—not turned loose upon a confiding community."

"Yet you say she is his own sister?"

"Yes, indeed! and the family have always been perfectly devoted to her! But they have sent her to the right-about now. It is too bad! A family row is such an unfortunate thing. They may be thankful not to have a murder-case to deal with!"

Strangely enough, I was *en route* for the house of my friend, Mrs. B., and as the car, at this juncture, crossed the street on which she lived, I motioned to the conductor to ring the bell, and alighted before hearing more of that remarkable tale. Being acquainted with the whole matter as it actually occurred, I was amused and indignant, as well as curious, to learn how this girl had received the wretchedly garbled version of an affair, the facts of which were these:

When Mr. B. was suddenly prostrated by an alarming attack of pneumonia, his sister, a noble woman who had taken up as her life-work the duties of a trained nurse in a Boston hospital, was telegraphed for. As she had a serious case in charge, it was impossible to obey the summons, and a New York nurse was engaged. Mr. B.'s physician had, early in his illness, prepared some powders, each containing a minute portion of morphine, and several had been administered to the patient. Of late, he had taken five grains of quinine each morning. A few days before the above mentioned harangue, the doctor ordered the nurse to double the usual dose of quinine. She, carelessly, or misunderstanding the directions, gave two of the morphine powders. The dose was not large enough to cause more serious injury than throwing the patient into a long and heavy sleep, and frightening his family. The doctor, who had engaged the nurse, discharged her, as Mr. B. was so far improved as to need only such care as his wife and daughter could give him.

My curiosity prompted me to inquire of Mrs. B. and Miss B., without divulging my motive, the particulars of the call they had received from the horse-car orator. I learned that Mrs. B. had told the girl's mother the facts of the case while the two daughters were talking together. Miss B. said that they, now and then, overheard a few words of the conversation between the older women, and that her companion had made several inquiries concerning it. Among others was the query:

"How many grains of the medicine does your father take every day?"

Miss B., supposing she referred to the quinine, answered:

"Five, generally; but on the day of which mamma speaks, ten grains were prescribed."

And from this scanty amount of rapidly acquired information had grown the story to which I had been an amazed listener.

"Behold how great a matter a little fire kindleth!"

Yet this girl did not intend to lie. She gleaned scraps of a conversation, and allowed a vivid imagination to supply the portions she did not hear. Add to this the love of producing a sensation, which is an inherent trait of many characters, and behold potent reasons for seven-tenths of the cases of exaggeration which come to our notice, romances constructed upon the "impressionist-picture" plan—a thing of splash and glare and abnormal perspective that vitiates the taste for symmetry and right coloring.

We all like to be the first to tell a story, and are anxious to relate it so well that our listeners shall be entertained. That a tale loses nothing in the telling is an established fact, especially if the narrator thereof observes a lack of interest on the part of his listeners. Then the temptation to arouse them to attention becomes almost irresistible and unconsciously one accepts the maxim at which we all sneer,—that it is folly to let the truth spoil a good story. Every day we have occasion to hold our heads, reeling to aching with conflicting accounts of some one incident, and repeat the question asked almost nineteen hundred years ago:

"What is truth?"

We hear much of people who are "too frank." These destroyers of the peace of mind of friend and foe alike pride themselves on the fact that they are "nothing if not candid," and "always say just what they think." Be it understood, this is not truthfulness. The utterance of unnecessary and unkind criticism, however honest, is impertinence, amounting to insolence.

When your "frank friend(?)" tells you that your gown does not fit, that you dress your hair in such an unbecoming manner, that your management of your household is not what it should be, she takes an unwarrantable liberty. If traced back, the source of these remarks would be found in a large percentage of instances, in a disagreeable temper, captious humors, and a spirit that is anything but Christian. One may be entirely truthful without bestowing gratuitous advice and admonition.

People differ widely in their notions of veracity, and few would endorse the technical definition with which this talk begins. Is it because there is so much intentional falsehood, so much that is not in "exact accordance with that which is, has been, or shall be," or that standards of veracity vary with individual disposition, and what may be classified as social climatic influences? Is it true that in morals there is no stated, infallible and eternal gauge—"the measure of a man—that is, of an angel?"

If a lie is something told "with the intention to deceive," as says the catechism, a nineteenth century Diogenes would have need to search in a crowd with an electric light in quest of a perfectly truthful man.

For our comfort and hope be it recorded that there are men and women who are uniformly veracious, and still courteous, who would not descend to falsehood or subterfuge, yet who are never guilty of the rudeness of making untactful speeches.

Were there more of such exceptions to the rule of inconsiderate, exaggerated and recklessly mendacious talk that wounds ear and heart, the "society lie" would be no more, and this flimsy excuse for falsehood would be voted an article too tenuous and threadbare for use.

Good people, so-called Christians, seldom appreciate what immense responsibility is theirs in setting the example of telling the truth, the whole truth and nothing but the truth. Said an amiable woman to me a few days ago:

"Mrs. Smith, who is a strict Sabbatarian, asked me yesterday if I had ever been to a Sunday reception or tea. Now, while I do not generally approve of them, I do, once in a great while, attend one. But, rather than shock her by acknowledging the offence I lied out of it. It is the only course left for the well-bred in such circumstances."

An hour later I saw her punish her child for denying that she had committed some piece of mischief of which she was guilty. The mother's excuse to herself probably was that the child told a lie, she, a "society fib." Perhaps the smaller sinner had no reputation for breeding to maintain.

The love for drink is not more surely transmitted from father to son than is the habit of lying. Once begun in a family, it rears itself, like a hooded snake, all along the line in generation after generation and appears to be an ineradicable evil. It spreads, too, as specks in a garnered fruit. We are startled by seeing it in children by the time they can lisp a lie, and we note in them, with a sickening at heart, the father's or grandfather's tendency to secretiveness or deceit, or the mother's *penchant* for false excuses. We can scarcely bequeath a greater sorrow to our offspring than to curse them before their birth with this hereditary taint, which is, perhaps, one of the hardest of all evils to correct. It may take the form of exaggerated speech, of courteous or cowardly prevarication, or of downright falsehood, but, in whatever guise, it is a curse to the owner thereof as well as to his family. If you are so unfortunate as to have any symptom of it in your blood, watch your boy or girl from infancy, and try, by all the arts in your power, fighting against nature itself, even, to prevent what is bred in the bone from coming out in the flesh.

We children of a larger growth can do much toward the correction of this blemish in others as in ourselves by close guard over our own speeches and assertions.

There are no sharper, more intolerant critics than the little ones, and if they inherit the tendency to insincerity the only way in which you can avert the much-to-be dreaded sin is by being absolutely truthful yourself. Cultivate veracity as a virtue, as a grace, as a vital necessity for the integrity of the soul. Prune excrescences in the shape of loose statements; if you err in telling a wonderful story, let it be in cutting down rather than in magnifying. A couple of ciphers less are better than one too many. It is to be feared that for many of us this would be a hard, although a wholesome task. The trail of the serpent is over us all. We yield heedlessly to the temptation to break promises, and to the habit of giving false reasons to our children, little thinking that their grave, innocent eyes may read our souls more clearly than those of older persons who are not so easily deceived by our tongues. When your child, although a mere baby in years, once discovers in you exaggeration or untruthfulness, he remembers it always, and you, from that moment, lose one of the most precious joys and sacred opportunities of your life— that of inspiring his entire confidence and trust, and of leading the tiny feet in the seldom-trodden path of Perfect Truth.

CHAPTER XXVI

THE GOSPEL OF CONVENTIONALITIES

Young people are proverbially intolerant, so I listened patiently, a few days since, to the outburst of an impetuous girl-friend.

"Oh," she exclaimed, "we are all such shams!"

"Shams?" I repeated, interrogatively.

"Yes, just that, shams through and through! We, you and I are no exceptions to the universal rule of, to quote Mark Twain, 'pretending to be what we ain't.' We are polite and civil when we feel ugly and cross; while in company we assume a pleasant expression although inwardly we may be raging. All our appurtenances are make-believes. We wear our handsome clothes to church and concert, fancying that mankind may be deceived into the notion that we always look like that. Food cooked in iron and tin vessels is served in French china and cut glass. When children sit down to table as ravenously hungry as small animals, their natural instincts are curbed, and they are compelled to eat slowly and 'properly.' You see it everywhere and in everything. The whole plan of modern society, with its manners and usages, is a system of shams!"

Marion Harland

In contradistinction to this unsparing denunciation, I place Harriet Beecher Stowe's idea of this "system of shams." In "My Wife and I" she says:

"You see we don't propose to warm our house with a wood fire, but only to adorn it. It is an altar-fire that we will kindle every evening, just to light up our room, and show it to advantage. And that is what I call woman's genius. To make life beautiful; to keep down and out of sight the hard, dry, prosaic side—and keep up the poetry—that is my idea of our 'mission.' I think woman ought to be what Hawthorne calls 'The Artist of the Beautiful.'"

Mrs. Stowe is in the right. In this commonplace, fearfully real world, what would we do without the blessed Gospel of Conventionalities? In almost every family there is one member, frequently the father of the household, who, like my young friend, has no patience with "make-believes" and eyes all innovations with stern disapproval and distrust. It is pitiful to witness the harmless deceits practiced by mothers and daughters, the wiles many and varied, by which they strive to introduce some much-to-be-desired point of table etiquette to which "Papa is opposed." Sometimes his protest takes the form of a good-natured laugh and shrug accompanied by the time-battered observation that "you can't teach an old dog new tricks." More frequently overtures of this kind are repulsed by the gruff excuse:

"My father and mother never had any of these new-fangled notions and they got on all right. What was good enough for them is good enough for me!"

And so paterfamilias continues to take his coffee with, instead of at the end of, his dinner, eats his vegetables out of little sauce plates with a spoon, insists that meat, potatoes and salad shall all be placed upon the table at once, and, if the father and mother than whom he does not care to rise higher were, in spite of their excellence, of the lower class, he carries his food to his mouth on the blade of his knife, and noisily sips tea from his saucer. Evidently he does not believe in shams, those little conventionalities, nearly all of which have some excellent cause for existence, although we do not always pause to examine into their *raison d'etre*. They may be founded upon hygienic principles, or on the idea of the greatest good to the greatest number. Many seemingly slight breaches of etiquette, if practiced by everyone, would create a state of affairs which even the most ardent hater of *les convenances* would deplore. If, for instance, all men were so entirely a law unto themselves that they despised the rule which commands a man to resign his chair to a lady, what would become of us poor women? In crowded rooms we would have the pleasure of standing still or walking around the masculine members of the company, who would sit at ease. Were the unmannerly habit of turning the leaves of a book with the moist thumb or finger indulged in by all readers, the probabilities are that numberless diseases would thus be transmitted from one person to another.

It argues an enormous amount of self-conceit in man or woman when he or she calmly refuses to conform to rules of etiquette. In plain language, we are none of us in ourselves *pur et simple* so agreeable as to be tolerable without the refinement and polish of manners upon which every "artist of the beautiful" should insist in her own house. Too many mothers and housekeepers think that "anything will do for home people." It is our duty to keep ourselves and our children "up" in "the thing" in table and parlor manners, dress and the etiquette of visiting, letter-writing, etc. Even among well-born people there are certain small tokens of good breeding which are too often neglected. One of these is what a college boy recently described in my hearing as the "bread-and-butter letter." At my inquiring look he explained that it was "the note of thanks a fellow writes to his hostess after having made a visit at her house—don't you know?"

This note should be written as soon as possible after the guest returns to her home, even if she has been entertained for only a night. In it she informs her hostess of her safe arrival, and thanks her for her kind hospitality. A few lines are all that is necessary.

It seems incredible that in decent society anyone should be so little acquainted with the requirements of the drawing-room as to enter a lady's parlor, and stop to speak to another person before first seeking his hostess and paying her his respects. And yet I have seen men come into a room and stop to chat first with one, then with another friend, before addressing the entertainer. If, while searching for the lady of the house in a parlor full of people, a man is addressed by some acquaintance, he should merely make an apology and pass on until he has found his hostess. After that he is free to talk with whom he pleases.

It is to be hoped that when a man commits the rudeness of passing into a room before a lady instead of giving her the precedence, it is from forgetfulness. Certainly I have frequently been the amazed witness of this proceeding. Forgetfulness, too, may be the cause of a man's tilting back his chair until it sways backward and forward, meantime burying his hands in the depths of his trousers pockets. But such thoughtlessness is, in itself, discourtesy. No man or woman has a right to be absorbed in his or her affairs to the extent of forgetting what is due to other people.

The tricks of manner and speech contracted by a boy or young man should be noticed and corrected by mother or sister before they become confirmed habits. Such are touching a lady on arm or shoulder to attract her attention, inquiring "What say?" or "Is that so?" to indicate surprise, glancing at the addresses on letters given him to mail, and consulting his watch in company. It would be difficult to find a better rule for courtesy with which to impress a boy or girl than the advice written by William Wirt to his daughter:

"The way to make yourself pleasing to others is to show that you care for them. The world is like the miller at Mansfield 'who cared for nobody, no, not he, because nobody cared for him.' And the whole world will serve you so if you give it the same cause. Let all, therefore, see that you do care for them, by showing what Sterne so happily calls 'the small sweet, courtesies of life,' in which there is no parade, whose voice is to still, to ease; and which manifest themselves by tender and affectionate looks, and little kind acts of attention, giving others the preference in every little enjoyment at the table, walking, sitting or standing."

There is one gross breach of good breeding which can hardly be due to inattention. There is a homely proverb to the effect that one "should wash her dirty linen at home," and it is to the violation of this advice that I refer. Discussing home matters, complaining of the actions of members of your family, or confiding their faults or short-comings to an outsider, even though she be your dearest friend, is as great an act of discourtesy as it is contrary to all the instincts of family love and loyalty. Your father may be a hypocrite, your mother a fool of the Mrs. Nickleby stamp, your brother a dissipated wretch, and your sister a professional shop-lifter, while your husband combines the worst characteristics of the entire family—but as long as you pretend to be on speaking terms with them, stand up for them against all the rest of the world; and if matters have come to such a pass that you have severed all connection with them, let a proper pride for yourself and consideration for the person to whom you are talking deter you from acknowledging their faults. These persons are members of your family—that should be enough to keep you forever silent as to their peccadilloes or sins. But, if you do not feel this, for politeness' sake refrain from making your listener supremely uncomfortable by your complaints. No true lady will so far forget her innate ladyhood as to be guilty of this rudeness.

To fulfill what Mrs. Stowe calls our "mission," we women must insist on the observance of the conventionalities at home. Husbands are sometimes, even when "taken young," too obstinate to change; although, to their credit be it said, if approached in the right way they will generally try to correct tricks of speech or manner. But with our children there should be no peradventure. Upon us is laid the responsibility of making them what we choose, of developing them into gentlemen, or neglecting them until they become boors. It is never too early to begin. First impressions are lasting ones, and the child who, from the beginning, is trained to observe the "small, sweet courtesies," not only when in company, but in the nursery and with the members of his own family, will never forget them. We often observe "that man does as well as he can, but he is not the gentleman born." That should, of itself, be a lesson to us mothers, to teach our children, not only by precept but by example, to keep alive the "altar-fire" of conventionality, and thus to make life warm, beautiful, poetic. After all, may not what the impulsive girl whom I quoted at the beginning of this talk termed the "sham" of life, be the real, though hidden side? We read that "the things which are seen are temporal; but the things which are not seen are eternal."

CHAPTER XXVII

FAMILIAR OR INTIMATE?

"What makes the difference between those two carriages?" I asked a wagon builder, while examining two light vehicles of the same general build and design. One cost twice as much as the other, and looked as if it were worth four times as much.

"Some of it is in the material, but more in the finishing," was the response. "This is of pretty fair wood, but simply planed and painted, while this"—pointing to the more costly equipage—"is as hard as a rock, and has been rubbed smooth, then polished until the surface is as fine as silk. Then it is flowed all over with the best varnish, left to dry ten days, and over-flowed again. That makes all the difference in the look of wagons. Two of them may be built just alike, and one will look like a grocer's errand-cart, while the other is a regulation gentleman's turnout. It is all the effect of polish and finish."

Involuntarily my mind reverted to Mr. Turveydrop and his modest assurance that "we do our best to polish, polish, polish."

The carriage builder struck the right chord when he affirmed that "finish made all the difference," and it applies as truly to flesh and blood as to insensate wood. Only the wood has sometimes the advantage of taking more kindly to improvement than do human free agents.

The rough places on which the effects of polish have not showed are too numerous for me to touch upon more than a few of them in this talk. We will acknowledge that the paint and varnish are not all that is necessary. The wood must be hard and prepared for the flowing process, if the wagon is to stand the scrutiny of critical eyes. Too often the paint is laid on thickly—perhaps too thickly—over indifferent material, and the first shock or scratch makes it scale and flake off.

As the test of the genuineness of the polish must be its durability, so intimacy is the standard by which we may judge of the finish of the so-called well-bred man or woman. If the refinement be ingrain, the familiarity which inevitably breeds contempt will never intrude itself.

To come down to everyday particulars: One of the unwarrantable familiarities is to enter a friend's house without ringing her door-bell,—unless you have been especially requested to do so. No ground of intimacy on which you and your friend may stand justifies this liberty. The housekeepers are few and far between who, in their inmost souls, will not resent this invasion of their domain. It argues an enormous amount of self-conceit on your part when you fancy that you are considered so entirely one of the family that your unannounced presence will *never* prove an unwelcome intrusion.

In country places neighbors contract the habit of "running in" to see one another. Were the truth known, many a housekeeper, deep in pie-making and bread-kneading, would gladly give her handsomest loaf for two minutes in which to smooth her rumpled hair and change her soiled apron.

It is only in books that the heroine always looks so charming, no matter in what labor she may be engaged, that she would be glad to receive any acquaintance. Of course our housewife's husband may see her when she is baking, and our domestic moralist would argue that what is good enough for him is good enough for callers. Perhaps it does not occur to her that the husband has so often found his wife dressed "neatly and sweetly" that the cooking costume will not make upon him the disagreeable impression it might produce upon a caller who sees her hostess once in this guise where the husband has hundreds of opportunities of beholding her in company clothes.

It may be remarked in this connection that the persons who are guilty of lapses like that of entering your front door unannounced are of the same class as those who enter your bed-chamber or sanctum without knocking. This is a rudeness which nothing warrants. There are times when we wish to be alone in our own rooms, and when we want to feel that we are safe from sudden interruption during the processes of bathing and dressing, even if the door of our apartment is not locked. One's own room should be so completely her own that her nearest and dearest will not feel at liberty to enter without permission. Of course it is frequently the case that two persons, sisters, or husband and wife, or mother and daughter, occupy the same chamber. When this is the case, it is *theirs* wholly and completely, and they are right to insist that other members of the household shall knock before entering.

Another evidence of lack of finish is offering gratuitous advice. If your opinion is asked, it is kind and right that you should give it; but a safe rule to go by is that unless your advice is requested it is not wanted. It is one of the strangest problems in human nature that one should of her own accord implicate herself in other people's affairs and take upon herself onerous responsibility by giving her unsolicited opinion in matters which do not concern her. It is a disagreeable task, and a very thankless one. Viewed from this standpoint, I am hardly surprised at the price demanded by lawyers for their advice. Perhaps the secret of their high fees may be that they decline to give a judgment unless asked for it. Our "own familiar friends" might learn a lesson from them.

It is a pity that any well-bred intimate should so far forget herself as to correct another person's child in the presence of the little one's father or mother. That this is frequently done will be certified to by hundreds of mothers who have been made irate by such untimely aids to their discipline. Johnny's mother tells him to stop making that noise, and her visitor adds severely, "Now, Johnny, do not make that noise any more!" Susie is saucy to her mamma, and her mamma's friend reprovingly remarks to the little girl that she is pained and surprised to hear her speak so naughtily to her dear mamma. Children resent this, and are far more keen and observant of these matters than their elders think.

Little four-year-old and his mamma were spending the day at grandpapa's last week. The family was seated on the veranda when the small man announced his intention to his mamma of going out upon the grass to pick wild flowers. Before the mother could reply, the grandfather stated his objection:

"No, child, the grass is too wet. I am afraid you will get your feet damp."

Four-year-old was equal to the occasion, as Young America generally is.

"Thank you, grandpa," was the calm response, "but my mamma is here. She can manage me."

Undoubtedly he was extremely impertinent; but did not the interference of the grandparent justify the rebuke?

Every one, even the lower classes, those who are considered under-bred, know that it is an atrocious impertinence to make inquiries of one's best friend as to the state of his finances. But like questions in the form of "feelers" are of such frequent occurrence that a reminder of this kind is scarcely out of place. There are few persons who deliberately ask you the amount of your income, but how often does one hear the queries:

"How much did you pay for that horse of yours?" "Was that gown very expensive?" "Have you a mortgage on that place?" "How much is the mortgage?" "What rent do you pay?" "How much does your table cost you per week?" etc., etc., until the unfortunate being at whom this battery of inquiries is aimed feels tempted to forget *his* "polish" and "finish," and retort as did the sobbing street boy when questioned by the elderly philanthropic woman as to the cause of his tears:

"None of your blamed business."

The etiquette of the table is supposed to be so thoroughly rooted and grounded into our children from infancy, and is, as a rule, so well understood by all ladies and gentlemen, that the visitor though a fool, could scarcely err therein. But this is not the case. At my own board, a man of the world, accustomed to excellent society, told me that he saw no mustard on the table, and as he always liked it with his meat he would trouble me to order some; while another man, a brilliant scholar, asked at a dinner party, "Will you tell your butler to bring me a glass of milk?" With these men the sandpaper of parental admonition or the flowing varnish of early association had evidently been neglected.

Intimacy, and even tender friendship may, and do, exist between men and women who are bound to one another by no family tie. Familiarity can never decently enter into such a relationship. If you, as a refined woman, have a man friend who slaps you on the back, squeezes your arm to attract your attention, holds your hand longer than friendship ought to dictate, and, without your permission, calls you in public or in private by your first name, you need not hesitate to drop him from your list of intimates. He is neither a gentleman nor does he respect you as you deserve. He may be, in his way, an estimable man, but it is not in *your* way, and he belongs to the rank of very ordinary acquaintanceship.

If a man asks you to call him by his first name, and your friendship with him justifies it, do not hesitate to do so; but if he is the "finished" article, he will not imagine that this concession on your part gives him the right to drop unbidden the "Miss" or "Mrs." from *your* name.

A true gentleman does not speak of a lady, even his betrothed, to strangers without what boys call "the handle" to her name. Nor should a woman mention men by their last names only. When a young or elderly woman speaks of "Smith," "Brown" or "Jones," you may make up your mind that the last coat of varnish was neglected when she was "finished."

Always be cautious in making advances toward familiarity. Be certain that your friendship is desired before going more than halfway. Not long ago I heard a woman say gravely of an uncongenial acquaintance whose friendship had been forced upon her:

"She is certainly my *familiar* friend. We can never be *intimate*."

CHAPTER XXVIII

OUR STOMACHS

In the best grades of society it is not now considered a sign of refinement to be "delicate." When our grandmothers, and even our mothers, were girls, robust health was esteemed almost a vulgarity. Now, the woman who is pale and "delicate" is not an interesting invalid, but sometimes an absolute bore. There are exceptions to this rule of pride in *in*delicate health,—notably among the lower classes. These people having neglected and set at defiance all hygienic rules, feel that a mark of special distinction is set upon them by their diseases. In fact, they "enjoy poor health," and take all occasions to discourse to the willing or disgusted listener upon their "symptoms," "disorders," their "nerves," and "Complaints." The final word should be spelt with a huge C, so important a place does it occupy in their estimation. The three D's which should be rigidly excluded from polite conversation—Domestics, Dress and Diseases—form the staple of their conversation. And the greatest of these is Diseases.

A farmer's daughter, whose rosy cheeks and plump figure elicited from me a gratulatory comment upon her robust appearance, indignantly informed me that she was "by no means strong, and had been doctorin' off and on for a year past for the malaria."

"Do you eat and sleep tolerably well?"

"Oh, yes," with the plaintive whine peculiar to the would-be invalid. "I sleep dreadful heavy. I take a nap each day for a couple of hours. And I must have a pound of beefsteak or mutton-chops for dinner. The fever makes me *that* hungry! You see it devours all that I eat, and the strength of the food goes to that."

Had any one pointed out to the deluded girl the folly of her theory, and explained that the fever patient becomes almost crazed from the restlessness that will not allow him to sleep, and that he loathes the very thought of food with a disgust that makes the daintiest dishes prepared by loving hands as gritty cinders between his teeth, she would have smiled patronizing superiority, and explained at length that her complaint was a peculiar one,—no common, everyday illness.

With this class, stomach disorders and their attendant sufferings, such as giddiness, shortness of breath and pain in the side, are always attributed to cardiac irregularity. There may be a lack of appetite and dull or acute pain following eating, and the fetid breath arising from a disordered condition of the stomach; but they resent the notion that their "heart disease" is dyspepsia, and would, in all probability, discharge the physician who recommended pepsin and judicious diet.

Perhaps the most discouraging feature of this class of persons is that they are ignorant and obstinate in this ignorance. The opinion of all the medical fraternity in the country would, in the farmer's daughter's estimation, be unworthy of consideration compared with the advice or suggestion advanced by one of her own kind. The practitioner among the unlearned has fearful odds to contend with in trying to bring an ignorant patient under his regimen. One word from sister, cousin or aunt, and the invalid will cast aside the physician's remedies, and take quarts of some patent medicine.

If you should question your laundress or cook, or your farmer's wife, you would be appalled to discover what peculiar notions she has of her physical make-up. It would be interesting and astounding to allow one of these people to draw a chart of her interior machinery, as she supposes it to be. It would bear as little resemblance to the reality as did the charts of the ancients who antedated Tycho Brahe, Pythagoras, and Copernicus, to the celestial charts of the nineteenth century. One would note especially the prominence given to certain organs. The stomach is almost, if not entirely, ignored. It is a matter for speculation why this valuable factor of the human system should be regarded with some disfavor by the ignorant. They joyfully admit the existence of the heart, brain and kidneys, and even the liver, and discourse with zestful unction on their own peculiar and special diseases of these organs; but suggest not to them that the stomach is out of sorts. This is not, in their estimation, a romantic Complaint. Their specialty is Nerves. To hear the frequency with which they attribute to these all uncomfortable sensations, one would imagine that the victims were made by a special pattern, like the tongue, of ends of nerves, all super-sensitive. The Nerves are a mysterious portion of their being, to whose account everything is laid, from extreme irritability and vexation, to nausea and rheumatism. "My nerves are *that* sensitive!" is a universal complaint.

It is difficult for the average mind to grasp the reason why the stomach, man's best friend and worst enemy, should be made of no account, and repudiated with such indignant resentment. Surely the giddiness occasioned by a tendency of blood to the head is no more romantic than the dizziness induced by gaseous fermentation of matter in the stomach.

The digestive organs should and do receive vast consideration from the medical profession. How often do we hear it said of some man lying at the point of death that as long as his digestive functions are duly performed there is hope; and how often, after the crisis is past, do we learn from the jubilant doctor that the patient's stomach was his salvation! "If *that* had failed, nothing could have saved him."

Let me recommend, as the pre-eminent duty of the sensible reader, care of the stomach and the alimentary apparatus. By care I do not mean dosing. With too many people the science of hygiene is confined in their imagination and practice to remedial measures. Of the weightier matters of precaution they reck nothing. Once in so often they "take a course of physic." This is done not so much because it is needed, as on principle, and because they have somewhere heard that it is a good thing to do. So, although all the digestive functions may be performing their part in a perfectly proper and regular manner, they must be weakened and irritated by draughts which do more harm than good.

Old proverbs are often the truest, and this may be affirmed of the adage that "an ounce of prevention is worth a pound of cure." Do not, if by care you can prevent it, allow your stomach to become disordered; but if, in spite of care, it is irritated, soothe instead of punishing it. Manage it as you sometimes control a fretful child,—by letting it severely alone. A few hours' fasting is an excellent remedy, and may continue until a feeling of faintness warns you that nature needs your assistance. Then eat *slowly* a little light food, such as milk-toast or very hot beef-tea. Quiet and diet work more wonders than quarts of medicine.

If your digestive organs are susceptible to disorder, be reasonably careful about what you eat, even though you

Marion Harland

consider yourself quite well. What a stomach has once done in the line of misbehavior, a stomach may do again. If a pitcher has in it a tiny flaw, it may crack when filled with boiling liquid. If you know of some article of food which disagrees with you, *let it alone*. If you are inclined to dyspepsia, eschew hot breads, pastry, fried or greasy food, nuts and many sweets. Avoid becoming dependent upon any medicine to ward off indigestion, if by care in your diet you can accomplish the same purpose. Many dyspeptics take an inordinate amount of bicarbonate of soda, an excellent corrective to acidity of the stomach when partaken of occasionally, and in small portions. In some cases, large and frequent doses have produced a cancerous condition of the coating of the stomach, which has resulted in death. It sounds ridiculous to speak of dependence upon soda-mint and pepsin tablets degenerating into an incurable habit, but there are some people to whom they are as necessary after each meal as were snuff and quids of tobacco to the old people seventy years ago.

Nature has provided a wonderful system of drains for carrying away the effete matter of the body. The effect caused by the neglect of these is akin to that produced by the choking of the waste-pipes in a house. If they become stopped, you send in haste for a plumber, that he may correct the trouble before it causes illness. If this state of affairs is allowed to continue in the human body, the system takes up the poison which slowly but surely does its work.

Next to the special organs designed for this plan of sewerage, the skin takes the most active part in disposing of impurities in the blood. The tiny pores are so many little doors through which the mischief may pass harmlessly away. But these pores must be kept open, and the only way to accomplish this end is by the free use of soap and warm water. This is such a homely remedy that it is sometimes sneered at and often overlooked. Certain portions of the body, such as the face and hands, are frequently washed, while other parts which are covered by the clothing are neglected. The entire body, especially in the creases where perspiration accumulates, should be sponged once a day, if one perspires freely. While sponging is excellent, a plunge bath should be frequently indulged in, as it opens the pores and thoroughly cleanses the entire surface.

Another desideratum is exercise, regular and abundant. Housework and walking are all that a woman needs, although she may find great pleasure as well as benefit from horseback riding, rowing and tennis. But let her not allow herself to tax her strength to the point of over-weariness. The amount of sleep needed by a woman is a mooted point, but unless she is what slangy boys term "constitutionally tired," she should sleep enough at night to ensure her against drowsiness in the daytime. For the elderly and feeble, an occasional nap after the noonday meal, especially during the warm weather, will prove most refreshing.

Try to bear in mind that you are not the only one concerned in your health. Higginson, in speaking of the duty of girls to observe all hygienic laws, tells us that, "unless our girls are healthy, the country is not safe. The fate of institutions may hang on the precise temperament which our next president shall have inherited from his mother."

CHAPTER XXIX

CHEERFULNESS AS A CHRISTIAN DUTY

Near me stands an anniversary present from a dear friend. It is a large "loving cup," and is just now full of my favorite nasturtiums—glowing as if they held in concentrated form all the sunshine which has brought them to their glory of orange, crimson, gold and scarlet. The ware of which the cup is made is a rich brownish-yellow in color, and between each of the three handles is a dainty design in white-and-cream, surrounded by an appropriate motto. The one turned toward me at present forms the text of my present talk and will, I hope, prove a happy hint to some of my readers:

"Be always as happy as ever you can,
For no one delights in a sorrowful man."

The rhyming couplet has set me to thinking, long and seriously, upon the duty of cheerfulness, a duty which we owe not only to our fellow-men, but to ourselves. It is such an uncomfortable thing to be miserable that I marvel that any sensible human being ever gives way to the inclination to look on the dark side of life.

In writing this article, I wish to state in the beginning that the women to whom it is addressed are not those over whom bereavement has cast dark shadows. For genuine grief and affliction I have vast and unbounded sympathy. For imaginary woes I have none. There is a certain class of sentimentalists to whom it is positive joy to be made to weep, and the longer they can pump up the tears the more content they are. These are people who have never known a heart-sorrow. They revel in books that end in death, and they listen to the details of a dying-bed scene with ghoulish interest. Had genuine bereavement ever been theirs, they would find only harrowing pain in such things. Shallow brooks always gurgle most loudly in passing over the stones underlying them. The great and mighty river flows silently and calmly above the large boulders hidden far below the surface.

The women of this sentimental class are those that read and write verses upon "tiny graves," "dainty coffins," and "baby shrouds."

The other day a friend shuddered audibly over the poem, admired by many, entitled—"The Little White Hearse."

"Just listen," she exclaimed, "to this last verse! After describing the grief of the mother whose baby has just ridden to what she calls 'its long, lasting sleep,' she further harrows up the feelings by winding up with:—

"I know not her name, but her sorrow I know—
While I paused on that crossing I lived it once more.
And back to my heart surged that river of woe
That but in the heart of a mother can flow—
For the little white hearse has been, too, at my door."

"How could she write it? How could she bring herself to put that down in black and white with the memory of the baby she has lost, in her mind?"

Marion Harland

"My dear," quietly answered a deep-natured, practical woman,—"either the author of that poem is incapable of such suffering as some mothers endure, or the little white hearse has never stopped at her door. If it had, she could not have written the poem."

She who "talks out" her pain is not the one who is killed by it. A peculiarity of hopeless cases of cancer is that the sufferer therefrom has a dread of mentioning the horror that is eating away her life.

Since, then, imaginary woe is a species of self-indulgence, let us stamp that healthful person who gives way to it as either grossly selfish or foolishly affected. Illness is the only excuse for such weakness, and even then will-power may do much toward chasing away the blue devils.

Some people find it harder than others to be uniformly cheerful. While one man is, as the saying is, "born happy," another inherits a tendency to look upon the sombre aspect of every matter presented to him. To the latter, the price of cheerfulness is eternal vigilance lest he lapse into morbidness. But after a while habit becomes second nature. I do not advocate the idea of taking life as a huge joke. The man or woman who does this, throws the care and responsibility that should be his or hers upon some other shoulders. My plea is for the brave and bright courage that makes labor light. When we work, let us work cheerfully; when we play, let us play with our whole hearts. In this simple rule lies the secret of the youth that endures long after the hair is white and the Delectable Mountains are in sight.

There is no habit of more fungus-like growth than that of melancholy, yet many good people give way to it. Some Christians go through this life as if it were indeed a vale of tears, and they, having been put in it without their consent were determined to make the worst of a bad bargain, and to be as wretched as opportunity would allow. How much better to consider this very good world as a garden, whose beauty depends largely upon our individual exertions to make it fair. We may cultivate and enjoy the flowers, or let them become so overrun with underbrush that the blossoms are smothered and hidden under the dank growth of the evil-smelling and common weeds.

Said a clergyman to one of his depressed and downcast parishioners:

"My friend, your religion does not seem to agree with you."

Only a few chapters back I quoted from the Apostle of Cheerfulness—Dr. Holmes—that most quotable of men. But he expresses what I would say so much more clearly than I can, that once more I refer my readers to him. I do not apologize for doing so. This last one of the noble company of America's great writers, who have passed away during the last ten years, cannot be read too much or loved too dearly. Let us see, what he, as Autocrat of the Breakfast Table, has to say on this subject.

"Oh, indeed, no! I am not ashamed to make you laugh occasionally. I think I could read you something which I have in my desk which would probably make you smile. Perhaps I will read it one of these days if you are patient with me when I am sentimental and reflective; not just now. The ludicrous has its place in the universe; it is not a human invention, but one of the divine ideas, illustrated in the practical jokes of kittens and monkeys long before Aristophanes or Shakespeare. How curious it is that we always consider solemnity and the absence of all gay surprises and encounter of wits as essential to the idea of the future life of those whom we thus deprive of half their faculties, and then call blessed. There are not a few who, even in this life, seem to be preparing themselves for that smileless eternity to which they look forward by banishing all gayety from their hearts and all joyousness from their countenances. I meet one such in the street not infrequently—a person of intelligence and education, but who gives me (and all that he passes), such a rayless and chilling look of recognition—something as if he were one of Heaven's assessors, come down to 'doom' every acquaintance he met—that, I have sometimes begun to sneeze on the spot, and gone home with a violent cold dating from that instant. I don't doubt he would cut his kitten's tail off if he caught her playing with it. Please tell me who taught her to play with it?"

It is one of the unexplained mysteries of human nature that people receive their griefs as direct from the hand of God, but not their joys. Why does not a kind Father mean for us to profit by the one as much as by the other? And since into nearly every life falls more sunshine than shadow, why leave the sunny places and go out of our way to sit and mope in the darkest, dreariest shade we can find? I believe in the Gospel of Cheerfulness. It is your duty and mine to get every drop of cream off of our own especial pan of milk. And if we do have to drink skim milk, shall we throw away the cream on that account? If it were not to be used it would not be there. God does not make things to have them wasted.

All of us have our worries—some small, some great—and the strength and depth of our characters are proved by the way in which we meet the trials. Cheerfulness is God's own messenger to lighten our burdens and to make our times of joy even more bright and beautiful. Have you noticed how, as soon as you can laugh over a vexation, the sting of it is gone? And the best of it all is that you cannot be happy yourself without casting a little light, even though it be but reflected sunshine, into some other life.

William Dunbar, in 1479, said:

"Be merry, man, and take not sair to mind
The wavering of this wretched world of sorrow:
To God be humble, to thy friend be kind,
And with thy neighbor gladly lend and borrow;
His chance to-night, it may be thine to-morrow!
Be blyth in heart for any aventure,
How oft with wise men it has been said aforow,
Without gladness availes no treasure."

CHAPTER XXX

THE FAMILY INVALID

One of the most anomalous of the inconsistencies peculiar to human nature is that we who are flesh, and consequently liable to all the ills to which flesh is heir, should know so little about the manner in which to check or, at least, alleviate these miseries. In the average household the proper care of the sick is an unknown art, or one so little understood that illness would seem to be an impossible contingency.

The chamber of illness is at best a sadly uncomfortable place, and it is the duty of the nurse, be she a hireling or the nearest and dearest of kin to the prostrate inhabitant thereof, to be cognizant of the methods of tending and easing the unfortunate being during the trying period of his enforced idleness. Only those who have been confined to a sick couch can appreciate its many trying features. The looker-on sees a man or woman uncomfortable or in pain, lying in an easy bed, "the best place for sick folk," with nothing to trouble him beyond the bodily malease which holds him there. He is merely laid aside for repairs, and, if the observer be somewhat wearied and overworked, he is conscious of a pang of envy. But he does not think of the sleepless nights through which the monotonous ticking of the clock is varied only by the striking of the hours, each one of them seeming double its actual length; or of the aching head and limbs; the feverish restlessness which makes repose an impossibility; or—most trying of all—the dumb nausea and loathing of the food, which, as one poor woman complained of meals partaken in bed, "tastes of the mattress and covers!"

The member of the family who is laid low by illness should receive the first consideration of the entire household. Intelligent care and nursing will be of more benefit than medicines. An old poem, written over two hundred and fifty years ago, struck the right chord when it advised:

"Use three physicians: First, Dr. Quiet,
Then Dr. Merryman, and Dr. Diet."

Noise and disturbance of whatever description must be an unknown quantity in a sick room. There "Dr. Quiet" should hold undisputed and peaceful sway. Felt or soft kid slippers, devoid of any offensive squeak, should be worn, and loud tones and exclamations prohibited. On the other hand, do not whisper to any person who chances to be in the room. Whispering arouses the patient's curiosity and suspicions, and, if he be asleep, the sibilant sound will pierce his slumbers and awaken him. Let all remarks be made in a low-pitched undertone. Never, even at the risk of causing offence, allow discussion of any subject to occur in the presence of the invalid. You may imagine that he does not mind it, that his mind will be diverted; but the argument ended, there may be noticed a flush on the cheek and a rapidity of breathing that bodes ill. One admirable physician makes it a rule never to permit political or religious topics to be canvassed in the hearing of one of his "cases," as a wide experience has taught him that such matters cannot be talked of without causing some degree of excitement, and thus retarding the patient's progress on the road toward health. For the same reason, try, by every effort, to keep your charge from thinking of work which should be done, and of any possible inconvenience he may be causing. There never was, and never will be, a convenient time for a person to be ill, so, whenever it comes, resolve to make the best of it. There is no greater cruelty than that of allowing a sick person to imagine that, but for his ill-timed indisposition, you might be able to go here or there, or to do this or that. Under such an idea the couch becomes a bed of clipped horse-hairs to the helpless sufferer, and he feels himself to be a useless hulk. This unkindness is oftentimes unintentional, and due more to thoughtlessness than to deliberate hard-heartedness. To avoid causing such discomfort do not look worried or distracted while ministering to your patient's wants, and do not fussily "fly around" in straightening and setting the room to rights. Let everything be done decently and in order, rapidly and quietly.

Another desideratum of the chamber of illness is *cleanliness* in the minutest particular. When the disease permits it, the sick person should be sponged all over daily, the teeth cleansed and the hair brushed. Wash the face and hands often during the day, as this process rests and refreshes.

The same gown should not be worn day and night, and the sheets must be changed frequently. If practicable, place a lounge at the side of the bed and lift or roll the patient off upon that, and turn mattresses and beat up pillows before re-making the bed. If this cannot be done with safety, the sheets may be removed, and others adjusted, simply by moving the invalid from one side to the other of the bed, rolling up the soiled sheet closely to the body, and spreading on the clean one in its place. Then the patient may be moved back to his original place, and the fresh sheet spread on the other side of the couch.

Air the room often, covering the patient warmly for a moment while you let in a sluice of ozone. Do not allow the chamber to become overheated, or to grow so cold as to chill the hands and face. The sick person may wear over the shoulders a flannel "nightingale" or jacket, to leave the arms at liberty.

In preparing the tray of food, let everything be as dainty as possible. Use for this purpose your choicest china and whitest linen. One important rule with regard to food is, Give a very little at a time, and avoid vulgar abundance. The sight of the loaded plate will discourage a weak appetite, and the delicate stomach will revolt at the suggestion of accepting such a mass. A small bird, a neatly trimmed French chop, a bit of tenderloin steak, or tender broiled chicken, will be eaten, when, if two chops or half a steak were offered, not a mouthful would be swallowed. To the well and strong this may seem like folly, but let us, in our strength, pity and humor the weaknesses of those upon whom God has laid suffering. It takes all the ingenuity and tact which love can muster to make a sick-room tolerable, and food anything but distasteful.

A poor consumptive girl had fancied that she could eat a few raw oysters, and the physician cheerfully prescribed them. At his next visit he was met by the mother, who informed him with dismay that her daughter would not touch the delicacy—"her stomach turned against it the instant the dish was brought in."

"How many did you let her see?" he asked.

"Two dozen!"

"Which would have daunted a well man, madam!" said the wise man. "Give her *one* at a time—cold and crisp, upon your best china plate, and tell her that is all she can have for at least an hour. Make her think that her appetite is under restraint. This is in itself a stimulant."

The hint is valuable.

In administering medicine, be careful to follow the physician's directions as to quantity and time of taking. Do not prepare the dose in the presence of the patient, as it may make him exceedingly nervous to watch the dropping or pouring of the drug; and after it has been swallowed, put bottle and spoon out of sight.

In too many families there exists sinful ignorance as to what should be done in case of illness before the doctor arrives. If a child comes in from play, hoarse and feverish, with nausea and pain in the head, he is often allowed to sit or lie about the house until the disagreeable symptoms become so pronounced as to cause alarm, and the physician is summoned. The sufferer should have his feet soaked in hot water, be put to bed, and some anti-febrine like aconite administered until a slight perspiration is induced. Aconite is such deadly poison that the mother must be sure she knows just in what quantity to give it. The dose for a child from three to six years of age is half a drop in a teaspoonful of water, every hour until the feverishness disappears. Unless serious illness is beginning, the chances are that, under this treatment, the little one will be almost well by the next day.

Mothers would do well to make a study of children's ailments and their proper treatment. Above all, the matter of diet should be comprehended. It is appalling to see the conglomeration of indigestible substances which a sick person is allowed to eat. All children should be trained to take medicine, and to submit to any prescribed dietary without resistance.

To keep up your patient's courage be, or at all events seem, cheerful. Wise old Solomon, in his day, knew that a merry heart did good like a medicine, and the morsel of wisdom is no less true now than then. Such being the case, bring into the presence of the sufferer a bright face and undisturbed demeanor.

Much may be said on the other side of the question, *i.e.*, from the nurse's standpoint. There are patients *and* patients, and some of them are *im*patients. It is a pity for a sick person to allow himself to so far lose control over his temper and manners as to be disagreeable when all that tender care and nursing can do is his. But really ill people are seldom cross, and the tried nurse may take to heart the comforting thought that one rarely hears of a man dying in a bad humor. It is undoubtedly discouraging to have a patient turn away from a carefully prepared dainty with a shudder of disgust and revulsion. It may sound harsh to say it, but nobody, sick or well, has the right to do such an unkind and rude thing. Any one in extreme bodily discomfort cannot be always smiling and uttering thanks, but he can be gentle and appreciative of the efforts that are made toward mitigating his distress. On his own account, as well as for the sake of his attendant, he should keep up a semblance of cheerfulness, the moral force of which is great. On the part of patient and nurse there must be self control and forbearance, which if closely practiced may bring sunshine into the most darkly shaded chamber of suffering.

Marion Harland

CHAPTER XXXI

A TEMPERANCE TALK

(Frank and Personal.)

A correspondent sends me, under cover of a personal letter, this request:

"Will Marion Harland show her hand upon the temperance question? The occasional mention of wine, brandy, etc., in her cookery-books, and her silence upon a subject of such vital moment to humanity, may predispose many to doubt her soundness as to the apostle's injunction to be 'temperate in all things.'"

To clear decks for action, I observe that the text quoted by my catechist contains no "injunction" but an impersonal statement of the truth that "Every man that striveth for the mastery" (or in the games) "is temperate in all things." The apostle is likening the running and wrestling of the Olympic games to the Christian warfare, and throws in the pregnant reminder that he who is training for race or fight must, as he says elsewhere, "Keep his body under." The same rules hold good with the athlete of to-day. While training, he neither drinks strong liquors nor smokes.

The stringency of the regulation, I interject in passing, is a powerful argument laid ready to the hand of the advocates of total abstinence. A habit that so far injures the physical powers as to tell upon the action of heart, brains, lungs or muscles, must be an evil to any human being, however healthy.

The Chief Apostle, in another place, admonishes his neophytes to let their "moderation" be known of all men. The revised version translates the word "forbearance" or "gentleness." We will try to keep both texts in mind during the informal homily that is the outcome of the question put to my surprised self.

"Surprised," because in the course of thirty-odd years of literary life I have had so many opportunities of "showing my hand" upon this and other great moral issues, and have improved them so diligently that my readers should by now be tolerably familiar with the platform on which I stand. Not being a card player, and knowing absolutely nothing of the technicalities of the game, I am at a loss whether or not to look for an implication of underhand work in the phrase chosen by the inquisitor. If she means that I have kept aught back which that part of the reading public that does me the honor to be interested in my work has a right to know, I hope in the course of this paper to disabuse her mind of the impression.

As a means to this end, I wish to put upon record disapproval that amounts to detestation of the practice of drinking anything that, in the words of the old temperance pledge I "took" when a child, "will make drunk come." That was the way it ran. The Rev. Thomas P. Hunt, one of the best known temperance lecturers in America, used to make us stand up in a body and chant it, he keeping time with head and hand, and the boys imitating him.

"We do not think

Marion Harland

We'll ever drink
Brandy or rum,
Or anything that makes drunk come"

I have never changed my mind on that head. What I thought then, I *know* now, that for half a century I have seen what desolation drunkenness has wrought in our land. I never see a boy toss off his "cocktail," or "cobbler", or "sling," or by whatever other name the devil's brew is disguised, with the mannish, knowing air that proves him to be as weak as water, when he would have you think him strong as—fusel oil!—that I do not recall the vehement outburst in Mrs. Mulock-Craik's "A Life for a Life," of the old clergyman whose only son had filled a drunkard's grave:

"If I had a son, and he liked wine, as a child does, perhaps—a pretty little boy, sitting at table and drinking healths at birthdays; or a schoolboy, proud to do what he sees his father doing—I would take his glass from him, and fill it with poison—deadly poison—that he might kill himself at once, rather than grow up to be his friends' curse and his own damnation—a *drunkard*!"

I lack words in which to express my contempt for the petty ambition, rooted and grounded in vanity, that urges a young fellow to prove the steadiness of his brain by tippling what he does not want, or even like. For not one in fifty of those who take "nips" and "coolers," cared for the taste of the perilous stuff at the first or twentieth trial. He proved himself a man, one of the stronger parts of creation, by pouring liquid fire down his quailing throat until he could do so without winking. He swears and smokes cigarettes at street corners for the same reason.

"I *love* a dog!" exclaimed a lively young girl, patting a big St. Bernard.

"Would I were a dog!" sighed an amorous dude.

"Oh, you'll grow!" retorted the fair one, consolingly.

I feel like plagiarizing the saucy hit, in witnessing the desperate efforts aforementioned on the part of our mistaken boy. Sometimes (let us thank a merciful heaven that this is so!) he does grow out of the folly, and into manly self-contempt at the recollection of it. Often—ah!—the pity and the shame of it!

If somebody were to make it fashionable to take belladonna, aconite or prussic acid in "safe" doses, three, or six, or a dozen times a day in defiance of all the medical science in the world, the would-be man would never be content until he had overcome natural repugnance to the "bitters," and rate himself as so much higher in the scale of being by the length of time his constitution could hold out against the deadly effect of the potation—plume himself upon his superiority to men who killed themselves by taking a like quantity. To drink one glass of wine or spirits a day is to venture upon thin ice; when the one glass has become the three that our boy *must* have, it is but a question of time how soon the treacherous crust will give way.

Clearly, then—so clearly that it is difficult to see how anybody, however blinded by self-conceit, can fail to perceive it—the only safe thing is to let liquor as a beverage alone. The practice is, at the best, like kindling the kitchen fire every morning with kerosene. Insurance agents are slow to take risks upon property where this is the rule.

Nobody is so besotted as to ask, "Does dram-drinking pay?" There is not a sane man or woman in America who would hesitate in the reply, and the answers would all be the same.

If he is a fool who tempts the approach of appetite that

may—that does in seventy-five times out of one hundred—become deadly and incurable disease, what shall we say of the "strong head" that espies no sin in social convivialities with the weak brother? Let me tell one or two stories of the score that rush upon my memory with the approach to this part of my subject.

Forty years ago I sat down to the dinner-table of a man who stood high in the community and church. He was a liberal liver, as his father had been before him. That father had taken his toddy tri-daily for seventy years, and died in the odor of sanctity. They could do such things in that day, and never transcend the three-glass limit. My godly grandfather did the same, and was never one whit the worse for liquor in his life. *Their sons and grandsons cannot do it without ruining themselves, body and soul.*

I italicize the sentence. I wish I could write it in letters of fire over the door of every liquor saloon.

It may be the climate; it may be the high-pressure, fever-heated rate of modern living; it may as well be that those honest men who made their own apple whiskey and peach brandy, by their daily dram-drinking transmitted the taste which adulterated liquors, in the generation following, were to lash into uncontrollable appetite.

But to my story. My father, one of the first in his day to set the example of total abstinence "for his brethren and companions' sake," had spoke repeatedly in my presence of the harm done by social drinking, and what influence women could exert for or against the custom. So I declined wine upon general principles when it was offered by the courtly host. No verbal comment was made upon my singular conduct, but the pert fifteen-year-old son of the house took occasion to drink my health with a dumb grimace, and beckoned the butler audaciously to fill up his glass, and a distinguished clergyman, whose parishioner the host was, looked polite astonishment across the table at the girl who dared. He took his wine gracefully—pointedly, it seemed to me—an example imitated by his curate, a much younger man. When we returned to the drawing-room, the master of the house sought me out, and began to rally me upon the attentions of a young man in the company to myself, in such a fashion that my cheeks flushed hotly with indignant astonishment. Lifting my eyes to his, I saw that he was *drunk*! The horror and dismay of the discovery were inconceivable. The rest of the interview, which was ended by his wife's appearance upon the scene to coax him off to his room, left an indelible impression upon my mind. The Spartans had a way of "drenching" a helot with liquor, then parading him in his drunken antics before the boys of the town to disgust them with dram-drinking. My object-lesson was the more striking because I had honored the inebriate.

The eloquent rector read the burial service over him ten years ago. For over twenty years he had been a hopeless sot, beggared in fortune, wrecked in reputation—a by-word and a hissing in a town where he had once stood among the best and purest. He outlived his son, who drank himself to death before he was thirty.

Another and later experience was in a fine old farm-house in the Middle States. There had been a birthday celebration, and neighbors and friends gathered about a board laden with country dainties, and congratulated the worthy couple who presided over the feast upon the four stalwart sons who, with their wives and children, were settled upon and about an estate that had been for six generations in the family. Hale, merry fellows they were—a little more red of face and loud of talk than was quite seemly in a stranger's eyes, but industrious and "forehanded," and kind of heart to parents, wives and babies. After dinner we sat under the cherry trees upon the lawn, and one of the sons brought out a round table, another a tray of glasses, another a monster bowl of milk punch.

Everybody pledged the patriarch's health in the creamy potation except myself. Again, I acted upon general principles. Were I a wine-bibber I should never touch glasses with a young man, or offer him anything "that could make drunk come." Disliking spirituous draughts of all kinds, and with the object-lesson of my girlhood branded upon memory, I refused to taste the brimming glass, even when the pastor of the household, a genial "dominie," rallied me upon my abstinence. He offered gallantly, when he found me obdurate, to drink my share, and had his glass replenished by the reddest-faced and loudest-mouthed of the farmer-sons.

"*You're* the right sort, dominie!" he said, with a roar of laughter, filling the tumbler until it ran over and into the pastor's cuffs. Whereat the farmer laughed yet more uproariously.

One of the four young men died a while ago of delirium tremens, and not one of the other three has drawn a sober breath in years. The parents are dead, the old farm is sold, and the brothers are all poor. Rum has done it all.

I do not imply that either of these scenes had any marked influence upon the destiny of the slaves of appetite, except as they were encouraged to pursue a course tacitly approved by the wise and good. But I am thankful that I did not lend the weight of a straw to the downward slide. "Woe unto him that putteth the cup to his neighbor's lips!" says the Book of books. There might be subjoined, "Or helps to hold it there when the neighbor's own hand has lifted it!"

Had I my way, not one drop of intoxicating liquors should be sold, except by druggists, and then only by a physician's prescription. For—and here comes the answer to the second part of my querist's appeal—I hold that pure brandy, wine and whiskey are of inestimable value as medicine. I know that the judicious use of them as restoratives has saved many lives. I know, too, how nearly worthless they are where the system of the patient is used to them as daily or frequent beverages.

I hold, furthermore, that there is no sin or even danger—unless the taste be already enkindled—in the occasional use of them in the kitchen, as one would handle vanilla, lemon or bitter-almond flavoring extracts. I do not believe that a single drunkard was ever made by the tablespoonful of wine that goes into a half pint of pudding-sauce, or the wine-glassful that "brightens" a quart of jelly. Every house-mother knows for whom she is catering. If one of her family or guests already loves and craves the stimulant, it is prudent to omit it. The same man would be tempted by the wine of the consecrated cup. When the disease of inebriety has gone thus far she cannot save him, but she can look to it that her hand does not give the final touch, which is death.

I have written frankly, and I think temperately. I am not a "crank" upon this—I hope not upon any subject. I am a temperance woman who does not scruple to avow what is her practice, as well as her belief. That thousands of better people than I will think my creed goes too far, and as many that it stops short of temporal and spiritual safety, ought not to trouble me. Upon the individual conscience lies the responsibility of principle and action. Yet holding as I do that each of us is his brother's keeper, I lift my hand in protest against the crying sin of the age, and the mistaken toleration of good people with that which leads to it.

Marion Harland

CHAPTER XXXII

FAMILY MUSIC

Our grandfathers and our grandmothers were drilled in vocal music in the church or neighboring singing-school. In that day—and for twenty-five years later—almost every household possessed and made frequent use of the Boston Academy, the Carmina Sacra, the Shawm and other collections of vocal music adapted for the use of societies and churches. Nearly everybody sang by note, and she was dull of ear or wits who could not bear her part at sight in any simple church tune. The pianoforte took the place of our grandmother's spinet and harpsichord, and every girl in every family was taught to play upon it after a fashion. She who had not taste or talent for music gave it up after her marriage. In this particular she was no more derelict than the "performer" of our times, whose florid flourish of classic music costs thousands where her grandmother's strumming cost hundreds.

The musical education of the girl of that period hardly deserved the name. The national ear for music, like the national eye for painting and sculpture, has made marvelous progress in fifty years. The singing school has gone to the wall along with the volunteer choir and the notion that every boy and girl can and ought to sing. Once in several whiles you find a "music-mad family," of which every member plays upon some instrument and studies music with expensive professors. Or one child displays what relatives rate as musical genius, and is educated to the full extent of the parent's ability. This done, the proficient becomes, in his or her own opinion, a privileged prodigy. Critical from the outset of his musical career, he grows intolerant of amateur work and disdainful of such compositions as the (musically) unlearned delight to honor.

"Don't you suppose," said the late Mrs. Barrow (the dearly-beloved "Aunt Fanny" of a host of little ones) to me at an evening *musicale*, "that seven out of ten professed disciples of the Wagner cult here present would, if they dared be unfashionable and honest, ask for music that has a tune in it rather than that movement in something flat or sharp to which they have seemed to give breathless attention for the last fifteen minutes?"

"A tune in it!" repeated a bystander in intense amusement. "Dear Mrs. Barrow, tunes are musical tricks, not true art."

This dogma, and others like unto it, are putting all our music-making into the hands of professional artists and hushing the voice of song and gladness in our homes. The one musician of the household is accredited with perfect taste and unerring judgment, and usually becomes a nuisance to his circle of acquaintances. He shudders at a false note; the woman who sings sharp is an agony, the man who flats is an anguish, and the mistakes of both are resented as personal affronts.

I know one girl (I wish I could stop at the singular number) who cannot enjoy going to her own church because the choir does not come up to her standard of perfection. She never sings in church herself. To mingle her voice with the tide of thanksgiving and praise would be like the crystal flash of the arrowy Rhone into the muddy Arve. She sets her teeth while ignorant and unfeeling neighbors join in the service of song, and confides on her way out of church to anybody who will listen to her that she really thinks it a misfortune to have as fine and true an ear as her own so long as people who do not know the first principle of music *will* persist in trying to sing. She has many companions in the persuasion that this part of the worship of the sanctuary should be left altogether to a trained and well-salaried choir. In the family honored by her residence there is no home music except of her making. There are, moreover, so many contingencies that may deprive her expected audience of the rich privilege of hearkening to the high emprise of her fingers and voice, that the chances are oftentimes perilously in favor of her dying with all her music in her.

Shall I ever forget, or rally from, the compassionate patronage with which she, a week agone, met my petition for

"When sparrows build and the leaves break forth?"

"I never sing ballad music," she said, loftily. "Indeed I could not do myself justice in anything this evening. I make it a matter of conscience not to attempt a note unless I am in perfect tune throughout—mentally, spiritually and physically. I should consider it an offence against the noblest of arts were I to sing just because somebody wishes to hear me."

This is not entirely affectation. The tendency of her art-education has been to make her disdainfully hypercritical. It has not awakened the spirit of the true artist, who is quick to detect whatever promises excellence and encourages the tyro to make the best of his little talent.

With all our newly-born enthusiasm for German composers, we have not taken lessons from the German people in this matter of home music. We do not even ask ourselves what has made them a musical nation. At the risk of writing myself down a hopeless old fogy, I venture the opinion that we were more nearly upon this track when the much-ridiculed singing-school was in full swing and every child was taught the intervals and variations of the gamut, and ballads were popular and part-songs by amateurs a favorite entertainment for evenings at home, than we are in this year of our Lord. The pews in that age united with a volunteer choir in singing with the spirit and with the understanding. The few may not have played their part as well as now, but the many did their part better. In the family, Jane may have surpassed her sisters in musical talent and proficiency, but one and all knew something of that in which she excelled, enjoying her music the more for that degree of knowledge. This brings forward another argument for the musical education of the masses, large and small. It would make general and genuine appreciation of good music, and put an end to the specious pretences of which we spoke just now. The German artisan's ear and voice are cultivated from childhood; his love of music is intelligent, his enjoyment of it hearty, yet discriminating.

Our babies hear few cradle songs under the new *regime*, except such as are crooned, more or less tunelessly, by foreign nurses. Girls no longer sing old ballads in the twilight to weary fathers and allure restless brothers to pass the evening at home in innocent participation in an impromptu concert, the boys bearing their part with voice and banjo or flute. We did not make perfect music when these domestic entertainments were in vogue, but we helped make happy homes and clean lives.

We used to sing—all of us together—upon the country porch on summer nights, not disdaining "Nelly Was a Lady" and the "Old Kentucky Home," and sea songs and love songs and battle songs that had thundering choruses in

Marion Harland

which bassos told mightily. Moore was in high repute, and Dempster and Bailey were in vogue. The words we sang were real poetry, and so distinctly enunciated as to leave no doubt in the listener's mind as to the language in which they were written. We had not learned that tunes were musical tricks. Better still were the Sunday evenings about the piano, everybody lending a helping (never hindering) voice, from grandpapa's cracked pipe down to the baby's tiny treble. Every morning the Lord of the home heard "our voices ascending high" from the family altar, and in the nursery feverish or wakefully-fretful children were lulled to health-giving slumber by the mother's hymns.

These are some of the bits of home and church life we would do well to bring forward and add to the more intricate sum of to-day's living. Granted, if you will, that we have outgrown what were to us the seemly garments of that past. Before relegating them to the attic or ragpicker, would it not be prudent and pleasant to preserve the laces with which they were trimmed?

CHAPTER XXXIII

FAMILY RELIGION

We are living in an age of surprising inventions and marvelous machinery. As a natural sequence, ours is an age of delegation. The habit of doing nothing by hand that can be as well done by a machine begets the desire to seek out new and presumably better methods of performing every duty appointed to each of us. Fine penmanship is no longer a necessity for the clerk or business man; skill with her needle is not demanded of the wife and mother. Our kitchens bristle with labor-saving implements warranted to reduce the scullion's and cook's work to a minimum of toil.

An important problem of the day, involving grave results, is founded upon the fact that, with the countless multiplicity of Teachers' Helps and Scholars' Friends, International Lesson Papers, Sunday-school weeklies and quarterlies and the banded leagues of associated youth whose watchword is "Christ and the Church," the children and young people of to-day are, as a rule, less familiar with the text of Holy Writ, with Bible history and the cardinal doctrines which the Protestant Church holds are founded upon God's revealed Word than were the children and youth of fifty years ago. Let me say here that I am personally responsible for this statement and what is to follow it. Having been a Bible-class teacher and an active worker in religious and charitable

Marion Harland

societies for forty years, and numbering as I do between twenty-five and thirty clergymen among my near kinsmen, I do not speak idly or ignorantly upon this subject. My appeal for corroboration of my testimony is to my contemporaries and co-workers.

The superficiality and glitter that are the bane of modern methods of education in our country have not spared sanctuary ordinances and family religion. "The church which is in thy house" is an empty form of speech when applied to a majority of so-called Christian homes. Early trains and late dinners, succeeded by evening engagements, have crowded out family prayers, and the pious custom, honored in all ages, of "grace before meat," is in many houses disregarded, except when a clergyman is at the table. Then the deferential bend of the host's head in the direction of the reverend guest is rather a tribute to the cloth than an acknowledgment of the Divine Giver to whom thanks are due. In the olden days it was the pupil who studied the Sunday-school lessons as needfully as he conned the tasks to be prepared for Monday's schoolroom. The portion of the old Union Question Book appointed for next Sunday was gone over under the mother's eye, the references were looked up, the Bible Dictionary and Concordance consulted. Then a Psalm or part of a chapter in the New Testament was committed to memory, and four or five questions in the catechism were added to the sum of knowledge to be inspected by the Sunday-school teacher and "audited" by the superintendent.

In writing the foregoing paragraph a scene arises before me of my father's fine gray head and serious face as he sat at the head of the room, Bible and reference books upon the stand before him; of the dusky faces of the servants in the background, intent upon the reading and exposition of the Word as they came from the lips of the master of the household, who for the hour was also the priest. I hear much, nowadays, of the "hard lines" that fell to the children of that generation, in that they were drilled after the manner I have described, and compelled to attend church twice or three times on Sunday. I affirm fearlessly that we did not know how badly off we were, and that the aforesaid "lines" seemed to our unsophisticated imaginations to be cast to us in pleasant places. The hour devoted each Sunday evening to the study of next Sunday's lesson was full of interest, the prayer that preceded it and the two or three hymns with which the simple service closed, gave it a solemnity that was delight, not boredom.

"Primitive methods" we call those studies now, and contemn, gravely or jeeringly, the obsolete practice of "going through" the Bible yearly by reading a given number of chapters every day. We assume that those were mechanical contrivances which, at the best, filled the mind with an undigested mass of Biblical matter and made sacred things trite. They who censure or sneer take no exception to the story that Demosthenes translated the works of Thucydides eight times, and also committed them to memory, that his style might be informed with the spirit and tone of his favorite exemplar. We cannot do away with the pregnant truth that the Bible-reading child of 1845 so steeped imagination and memory in the Holy Word that the wash of years and the acids of doubt have never robbed him of it. The Psalms and gospels then learned stay by us yet, responsive to the prick of temptation, the stroke of sorrow, the sunlight of joy. When strongly moved we unconsciously fall into Scriptural phraseology. God's promises then learned are our song in the house of our pilgrimage. We do not confound patriarchs with prophets, or passages from the epistles with the Psalms of David.

I am continually confronted by illustrations of the truth that the "contract system" prevails in religious teaching as extensively as in the manufacture of garments and food and furniture, and that the results in all cases are the same. Machine work cannot compare in neatness and durability with hand-made goods. The complaint, "I cannot get my Bible class to study the lessons," is almost universal. I have known large classes of adults to be made up with the express proviso that none of the members should be expected to prepare the lesson. Their appearance in the classroom at the stated hour fulfills their part of the compact. In thus presenting themselves they "press the button." The teacher does the rest. The mother, taking her afternoon siesta, or reading her Sunday novel at home, rarely knows the subject of the Bible lesson, much less what the teacher's treatment of it is.

I do not mention the pastor purposely. Except when he sees them in the Sunday-school, the faces of the children belonging (by courtesy) to his cure of souls are seldom beheld by him. The Sunday-school originally intended for the neglected children of the illiterate poor, has come to be the chief instrumentality upon which well-to-do church members depend for the spiritual upbuilding of those who are to form the church of the future. If one is tempted to challenge the assertion, let him compare the number of children (not infants) enrolled in our Sunday-schools with those who habitually attend upon divine service. The absence of the sunny, restless polls from the rows of worshipers in the pews, the troops of boys and girls who wend their way homeward at the conclusion of the Sunday-school exercises are accounted for by so-called humane apologists by the plea that two services in one day are burdensome to the little folk. And mothers "enjoy the service far more when they are not disturbed by fidgety or drowsy children." "Then, too, much of the sermon is unintelligible to them. Why torture them by a mere form?"

An old-fashioned clergyman—a visitor to a city church which I chanced to attend last winter—prefaced his sermon, "as was his custom at home," he said, by "a five-minute talk to the lambs of the fold." In the congregation of at least 800 souls there were exactly three "lambs" under fifteen years of age. It was impossible for the most reverent of his hearers to help thinking of the solitary parishioner who composed his pastor's congregation upon a stormy day, and objected to the sermon dutifully delivered by the minister "as good, but too personal."

It is as impossible for the thoughtful student of the signs of the times to avoid the conclusion that the growing disposition of the young to deny the authority of the church and to supersede her stated ordinances by organizations established and run by themselves may be the legitimate fruit of the prominence given by their parents to what should be the nursery of the church over the church itself. It would be strange if, after witnessing for fourteen or fifteen years such open and systematic disrespect of the gates of Zion, they were to develop veneration for her worship and devout appreciation of the mystic truth that this is the place where God's honor dwells.

If—and the "if" is broad and deep and long—the little ones are faithfully trained by the parents in the nurture and admonition of the Lord (dear, quaint old phraseology, fine, subtle and pervasive as lavender scent!), if sacred songs and Bible stories and tender talk of the Saviour's love and the beautiful life of which this may be made a type and a foretaste, keep in the minds of the little ones at home the sanctity and sweetness of the day of days, there is a shadow of excuse for the failure to make room for them in the family pew. Even then the tree will grow as the twig is inclined.

The mother whose knee is the baby's first altar, who gathers about her for confession, for counsel and for prayer sons and daughters who will, in older and sterner years, call her

Marion Harland

blessed for the holy teachings of their childhood, will teach them to find, with her, the tabernacles of the Lord of Hosts "amiable," *i.e.*, worthy of all love and fidelity. The chrism of motherhood consecrates a woman as a priestess. Neither convenience nor custom can release her from the office. Let not another take her crown.

CHAPTER XXXIV

A PARTING WORD FOR BOY

Upon the satin seat of a chair in the corner of the drawing-room, lie six white Lima beans, and three small red-spotted apples. Wild fruit they are, cast by a superannuated crab, spared by the woodman's axe because it stands on the verge of the orchard. The apple-pickers never look under it for gleanings. The beans were pulled from a frost-bitten vine in the garden, and shelled with difficulty, the pods being tough, and Boy's fingers tender. Both trophies secured, they were brought into the house, deposited in the safest place Boy's ingenuity could devise, and, alas! forgotten in the hurry of catching the "twain." There was no room for them in Boy's long-suffering pockets. They bulged to the bursting point with chestnuts, also the spoil of the grasping little fingers.

Boy is city-born and city-bred, and a day in the country is better than a thousand in street and park. A day in the woods, when chestnuts and walnuts hustle down with every breath of air, and the hollows are knee-deep with painted leaves, has joys the eager tongue trips over itself in the endeavor to recount. Boy and Boy's mother took the six o'clock train to town last night. This morning, throwing open the parlor blinds, I espy the six flat, white beans and the three red-speckled crab-apples. They were so much to

Marion Harland

the owner; except for the value imparted by association with the dancing blue eyes and the tight clutch of fingers that had green stains on them when the wrestle with the pods was over, they are so much more than worthless to everybody else—that there is infinite pathos in the litter. It is picturesque and poetic.

There will be no poetry, picturesqueness or pathos in the litter when Boy is older by a year or two. His leavings in outlandish places will become "trash," and still later on "rubbish" and "hateful." At twelve years of age he will be a "hulking boy," and convicted of bringing more dirt into the house upon one pair of soles than three pairs of hands can clean up. Eyes that fill now in surveying the tokens of his recent occupations and his lordly disregard of conventionalities, will flash petulantly upon books left, face downward, over night, on the piazza floor; muddy shoes kicked into the corner of the hall; the half-whittled cane and open knife on the sofa, and coats and caps everywhere except upon the hooks intended for them.

I once heard a grown-up beauty declare in the presence and hearing of a half-grown brother, that, "every boy should be put under a barrel at fourteen, and kept there until he was twenty, out of the sight of his kindred and acquaintances."

"Up to twenty-one he is an unmitigable nuisance!" concluded the belle, with the vanity of one who has put the case smartly.

The lad listened to the tirade without the twitch of a muscle—stolidity that proved him to be well used to such flaying. Three out of four boys in that family "turned out badly," and were cried down by a scandalized community for disgracing a decent and godly ancestry. Hearing this, I recollected the beauty and the barrel, and speculated sadly whether or not this were the key to the enigma.

It generally happens that the grown-up sister has less patience with the growing brother than any other member of the household. From principle and from inclination, and, I am inclined to add, from nature, she "sits upon" Boy habitually.

Ungrateful Lady Mary Wortley Montagu called her quondam lover, Alexander Pope—

> "A sign-post likeness of the human race:
> That is, at once resemblance and disgrace."

In her visions of the coming man, the sister resents the truth that Boy belongs to the same species and sex, or persists in judging him by this standard. In the "freshness" of his age and kind, he is skeptical as to her good looks and other fascinations, and takes wicked satisfaction in giving her to understand that he, at least, "is not fooled by her tricks and manners." If her "nagging" is a thorn under his jacket, his cool disdain is a grain of sand inside of her slipper.

What looks like natural antipathy between big sisters and little brothers is but one of several reasons why home is so often less like home to the boys than to the rest of the family.

I have in my mind's eye a distinct picture of the quarters allotted to a promising college-lad in the mansion of a wealthy father, and which I saw by accident. Each of the three accomplished sisters had her own bed-chamber, fitted up according to her taste. A spacious sitting-room on the second floor, with windows on the sunny front and at the side, was common to the trio. There were flowers, workstands, desks, easels, bookshelves, lounging and sewing chairs, pictures selected by each; *portieres* in the doorways and costly rugs upon the polished floor. Up two flights of stairs, *on the same floor with the servants*, the brother was domiciled in a low-browed, sunless back-room, overlooking kitchen-yards and roofs. A dingy ingrain carpet was worn thin in numerous places; no two pieces of furniture were even remotely related to one another in style or age. The wall-paper hung here and there in strips; the windows were dim with dirt; dust lay thickly in every corner; a counter-pane of dubious complexion had a dark, wide-spreading stain in the centre.

It is true, I admit, that the place reeked with stale cigar smoke, and that the infirm table propped for security against the wall, groaned under a collection of juvenile "properties," the heterogeneity of which, defies my pen and memory. But, bestow a wild boy in such lodgings as he might find in a low tavern, and he will treat them accordingly. He is more observant than his mother imagines, and more sensitive than his sisters would believe. Too proud to betray the sense of humiliation engendered by appointments unsuited to his station and education, he proceeds to be "comfortable" and "jolly" in his own way.

To return to our own Boy—who, my heart misgives me, lifted up his voice and wept sore last night upon discovering that the hard-won beans and scarlet-speckled apples were left behind—his loving mother has hung his nursery walls with good engravings and artistically-colored pictures, in the conviction that a child's taste for art is formed early and for long. Heaven grant that she may keep true to this principle in all matters pertaining to his upbringing, and in judicious dependence upon the influence of external impressions upon the immature mind of her offspring!

Is our bigger boy, then, so rooted and grounded in right tastes and right feeling as to be proof against the atmosphere of the worst-located and worst-furnished room covered by his father's roof? How far will the mother's assertion that he is the apple of her eye and dearest earthly possession go, when balanced against the object-lesson of quarters which are the household hospital of incurables, in the line of beds, tables, stools and candlesticks? If his sister's room is adorned with exquisite etchings and choice paintings, while his is the refuge for chromos that have had their day—will he not draw his own inferences? If his mother never climbs to the sky-parlor to see that the careless housemaid does her duty in sweeping, dusting and picking-up, does not he divine why his chamber is systematically neglected?

Many a shrewd fellow has marked the progress of an ageing or shabby article of furniture, from the guest-chamber, through the family rooms upward, until it settles for life, or good behavior, in his apartment, and felt a dull pang at heart that he would not confess. Many another fellow, as shrewd and more reckless, has flung out passionately at what he construed into an insult, and made it the ostensible excuse for resorting to places where the motto that "anything will do for the boys," is unknown in practice.

An English woman once commented to me upon the difference between our manner of lodging and treating our sons and that which obtains in her native land. "We behave to our boys as if they were princes of the blood," she said, in her soft, sweet voice. "American girls are young princesses at home and in society, and grace the position rarely well. But—excuse me for speaking frankly—their brothers are sometimes lodged like grooms."

She was so far from wrong that I could not be displeased at the blunt criticism. The just mean between the stations thus specified is equality, and the firm maintenance of the same by the parents. Manners and environment are apt to harmonize. To teach a boy not to be slovenly and destructive in his own domain, give him a domain in which he can feel the pride of proprietorship. He would like to invite his comrades into his "den," as his sisters entertain intimate friends in their boudoir. He may not put into words the reasons why, instead of saying openly—"Come in and up!" to his evening visitor, he whispers at the outer door, "Let us go out!" which too often means, also, "down." Perhaps he is so imbued with the popular ideas respecting the furnishment of his lodging-place as hardly to interpret to himself his unwillingness to let outsiders see how well his "den" deserves the name.

Nevertheless, fond mother, give him the trial of something better. Send the "incurables" to the auction room, and fit him out anew with what should be the visible expression of your love and your desire for his welfare. Why expect him to take these on trust any more than you expect the daughters to do this? Yet their apartments are poems of good-will and maternal devotion.

In all sincerity, let me notify you that the son will not keep his premises in such seemly array as the girls keep theirs. It is not in the genuine boy. I question if a three-year-and-a-half-old granddaughter would have chosen as a safe place of deposit for the white beans and red-freckled apples the handsomest chair I have. You will find your laddie's soiled collars in his waste-paper basket; his slippers will depend from the corner of the picture you had framed for him on his last birthday; his dress-suit will be crumpled upon his wardrobe shelf, and his *chiffonier* be heaped with a conglomeration of foils, neckties, dead *boutonnieres*, visiting-cards, base-balls, odd gloves, notebook, handkerchiefs, railway guides, emptied envelopes, caramel papers, button hooks, fugitive verses, blacking brushes, inkstand, hair brushes—the mother who reads this can complete the inventory, if she has abundant patience, and time is no object with her.

Nevertheless, I repeat it—let him have his "den," and one in which he can find more comfort and enjoyment than in any other haunt. We mistake—the most affectionate of us—in attributing to our sons' sensibilities the robustness or wiry insensitiveness that belongs to their physical conformation. Timely gifts are not thrown away upon them; each tasteful contribution to their well-being and happiness is a seed set in good soil.

A dear friend, in whose judgment I have put much faith, put it well when she gave her reason for rectifying only the glaring disorders of her boy's apartments while he was out of them, and letting the rest go.

"They must be clean and bright," she remarked, with tender forbearance. "But I never meddle with his books and papers, or do anything that will, in his opinion, mar the individuality of his quarters. He likes to feel that they have the impress of himself, you see. Rigid surveillance, or the appearance of it, would irk him. For a long time it annoyed me that he preferred his imprint to mine. A pile of pamphlets on the carpet within easy reach of his chair was a grievance; his boxing gloves were an eyesore when left upon his table, and he *might* find some other place for his dumb-bells than the exact middle of the room. Then, by degrees, I thought my way to the stable verity whereupon I now rest, that *the boy is worth more than the room.*"

CHAPTER XXXV

HOMELY, BUT IMPORTANT

The French woman dresses herself with a view to pleasing the cultivated eye. She consults her complexion, height, figure and carriage, in color, make and trimming. Her apparel partakes of her individuality.

The American woman wears her clothes, as clothing, and has them made up of certain materials and in various ways, because dressmakers and fashion-plates prescribe what are this season's "styles."

Dissimilarities as marked prevail in the cookery of the two nations. Daintiness and flavor take the rank of other considerations with the French cook; with the American,— *fillingness*! I can use no substitute for the word that will convey the right idea.

The human machine (of American manufacture) must be greased regularly and plied with fuel or it will not go. And "go" is the genius of American institutions. Cookery with us is means to an end; therefore, as much a matter of economy of time and toil as building a road. Almost every cottage has specimens of fine art on the walls in the shape of pictures "done" by Jane or Eliza, or embroidery upon lambrequin, *portiere*, or tidy. It occurs to Jane and Eliza as seldom as to their fore-mothers, that cooking is an art in itself, that may be "fine" to exquisiteness. In their eyes, it is an ugly necessity, to be got over as expeditiously as "the men-folks" will allow, their coarser natures demanding more and richer filling than women's. It follows that dishes which require premeditation and deft manipulation are unpopular. The scorn with which our middle class woman regards soups, jellies, salads and *entrees* is based upon prejudice that has become national. Recipes marked—"Time from three to four hours," are a feature of English cook-books. We American writers of household manuals are too conversant with Jane's and Eliza's principles to imperil their sale by what will be considered danger-signals. This same desire to dispatch a disagreeable task increases in said manuals the number of "Quick Biscuit," "Minute Muffins" and "Hasty Pudding" recipes.

Represent to the notable housewife who is scrupulous in saving minutes, candle-ends and soap grease, that a few pounds of cracked bones, a carrot, a turnip, an onion and a bunch of sweet herbs, covered deep with cold water, and set at one side of the range on washing-day, to simmer into soup stock, wastes neither time nor fuel and will be the base of more than one or two nourishing dinners; prove, by mathematical demonstration, that a mold of delicious blanc-mange or Spanish cream or simpler junket costs less and can be made in one-tenth of the time required for the leathery-skinned, sour or faint-hearted pie, without which "father'n the boys wouldn't relish their dinner;" that an egg and lettuce salad, with mayonnaise dressing, is so much more toothsome and digestible than chipped beef as a "tea relish," as to repay her for the few additional minutes spent in preparing it—and her skeptical stare means disdain of your interference, and complacent determination to follow her own way.

She has heard that "country people in furren parts a'most

live upon slops and grass and eggs and frogs, and supposes that's the reason Frenchmen are so small and dark-complected." She thanks goodness she was born in America, "where there's plenty to eat and to spare," she adds, piously, as she puts the chunk of salt pork on to boil with the white beans, or the brisket of salt beef over the fire with the cabbage, before mixing a batch of molasses-cake with buttermilk and plenty of soda.

The corner-stone of her culinary operations might have been cut from the pillar into which another conservative woman with a will of her own, was changed. It is solid salt. Salt pork, salt beef, salt fish, relieve one another in an endless chain upon her board. She averts scurvy by means of cabbage and potatoes. I know well-to-do farmers' wives who do not cook what they call "butcher's meat," three times a month, or poultry above twice a year. Dried and salt meat and fish replenish what an Irish cook once described to me as "the *meat corner* of the stomach."

"Half-a-dozen eggs wouldn't half fill it, mem;" she protested, in defence of the quantity of steak and roast devoured daily below-stairs.

Our native housewife does not make the effort to crowd this cavity with the product of her poultry yard. Eggs of all ages are marketable and her pride in the limited number she uses in filling up her household is comic, yet pathetic. Cream is the chrysalis of butter at thirty cents a pound; to work so much as a tablespoonful into dishes for daily consumption would be akin to the sinful enormity of lighting a fire with dollar bills. She sends her freshly-churned, golden rolls to "the store" in exchange for groceries, including *cooking butter* to be used in the manufacture of cake and pastry.

These she *must* have. Appetites depraved by fats—liquid, solid and fried—crave the assuasives of sweets and acids.

"Hunky" bread-puddings and eggless, faintly-sweetened rice puddings, and pies of various kinds, represent dessert. Huge pickles, still smacking of the brine that "firmed" them, are offered in lieu of fresher acids. Yet she sneers at salads, and would not touch sorrel soup to save a Frenchman's soul. For beverages she stews into rank herbiness cheap tea by the quart, and Rio coffee, weak and turbid, with plenty of sugar in both. Occasionally the coffee is cleared (!) with a bit of salt fish skin. I was told by one who always saved the outside skin of codfish, after soaking it for fish balls, for clearing her coffee, that, "it gives a kind of *bright* taste to it; takes off the flatness-like, don't you know?" We raise more vegetables and in greater variety than any other people; have better and cheaper fruits than can be procured in any other market upon the globe; our waters teem with fish (unsalted) that may be had for the catching. Yet our national *cuisine*—take it from East to West and from North to South—is the narrowest as to range, the worst as to preparation, and the least wholesome of any country that claims an enlightened civilization.

Properly fried food once in a while is not to be condemned, as the grease does not have a chance to "soak in." But when crullers or potatoes or fritters are dropped into warm (not hot) lard, and allowed to remain there until they are oily and soggy to the core, we may with accuracy count on at least fifteen minutes of heartburn to each half-inch of the fried abominations.

Perhaps there is nothing in which we slight the demands of Nature more than in *what and how we eat.* Chewing stimulates the salivary glands to give out secretions to aid in disposing of what we eat. We swallow half-chewed food, thus throwing undue labor on the stomach. It is impossible for the work of disgestion to be carried on in the stomach at a temperature of less than one hundred degrees. Yet, just as that unfortunate organ begins its work we pour into it

Marion Harland

half-pints of iced water. We add acid to acid by inordinate quantities of sugar, and court dyspepsia by masses of grease. If we thus openly defy all her laws, can we wonder if the kind but just mother calls us to account for it?

CHAPTER XXXVI

FOUR-FEET-UPON-A-FENDER

It is the sisterly heart rather than the author's fancy that gives me as a companion in this, the last of these "Familiar Talks," the typical American house-mother.

Whatever the alleged subject discussed in former chapters—and each has borne more or less directly upon the leading theme, old yet never trite,—THE SECRET OF A HAPPY HOME,—I have had in heart and imagination this thin, nervous, intense creature whom I seat beside me. Her own hands have made her neat; the same hands and far more care than ever goes to the care of herself make and keep her home neat and comfortable.

The dying Queen of England gasped that after her death there would be found stamped upon her heart the name of the Calais lost to her kingdom in her reign. Our housewife carries her household forever bound upon her heart of hearts. The word is the hall mark upon every endeavor and achievement. It would be a poor recompense for a life of patient toil to convince her that she has wrought needlessly; that the same energy devoted to other objects would have made a nobler woman of her and the world better and happier. Nor am I sure that in a majority of instances this would be true. On the contrary, I hold religiously to the

Marion Harland

belief that God had wise reasons for setting each one of us in the socket in which she finds herself. "Be more careful," says an old writer, "to please Him perfectly than to serve Him much." If there are tasks which you, my sister, cannot demit without inconveniencing those whose welfare is your especial care, take this as a sure proof that the Father, in laying this work nearest to your hand—and not to that of another—has called you to it as distinctly as He called Paul to preach and Peter to glorify his Lord by the death he was to die.

In the talk we hold with our four feet upon the fender, the fire-glow making other light unnecessary, I do not propose to enter upon the favorite theme with some, of what you might have done had circumstances been propitious to the assumption of what are rated as more dignified duties. We will take your life as it is, and see what the practice of the inward grace I shall designate can make of it.

You are inclined to be down-hearted upon anniversaries. You need not tell me what I know so well of myself. Another year has gone, another year has dawned, and you are in the same old rut of ordering and cooking meals and clearing up after they have been eaten, sweeping, dusting, making and mending clothes, washing, dressing and training children, and the thousand and one nameless tasks that fritter away strength, leaving nothing to show for the waste.

"God help us on the common days,
The level stretches white with dust!"

prays Margaret Sangster. You would cry out in the pain of retrospection and anticipation, that all the days of the years of your life are common days—"only that and nothing more."

If this be so, you need the Help none ever seek in vain more than those to whom varied and exciting scenes are alloted.

The angel of death who had said upon entering the plague-stricken city that he meant to kill ten thousand people, was accused on the way out of having slain forty thousand.

"I kept my word," he answered. "I killed but ten thousand. Fear killed the rest!"

If work slays thousands of American women, American worry slays her tens of thousands. Work may bend the back and stiffen the joints. It ploughs no furrows in brow and cheek; it does not hollow the eyes and drag all the facial muscles downward. These are misdeeds of worry—your familiar demon, and the curse of our sex everywhere. A good man—who, by the way, had a pale, harassed-looking wife—once told me that on each birthday and New Year's he retired to his study and spent some time behind the locked door in making good resolutions for the coming year.

"I may not keep them all," he said, ingenuously, "but the exercise of forming them is edifying."

With the thought of his wan and worried wife in mind, I shocked him by declining for my part to undertake such a big contract as resolutions for a year, a month or a week. If I live to a good old age, I shall owe the blessing in a great measure to the discovery, years ago, that I am hired not by the job, but by the day. If you, dear friend, will receive this truth into a good and honest heart, and believing, abide in and live by it, you will find it the very elixir of life to your spirit.

Come down from the pillar of observation. You might enact Simeon Stylites there for twenty years to come and be none the wiser or happier for the outlook. Refuse obstinately to take the big contract. Let each morning and evening be a new and complete day. In childlike simplicity live as if you were to have no to-morrow so far as worrying as to its possible outcome goes. Make the best of to-day's *in*come. Not one minute of to-morrow belongs to you. It is all God's. Thank him that His hands hold it, and not your feeble, uncertain fingers.

Longfellow wrote nothing more elevating and helpful than his sonnet to "To-morrow, the Mysterious Guest," who whispers to the boding human soul:

> "'Remember Barmecide,
> And tremble to be happy with the rest.'
> And I make answer, 'I am satisfied.
> I know not, ask not, what is best;
> God hath already said what shall betide.'"

The new version of the New Testament, among other richly suggestive readings, tells us that Martha was "*distracted* with much serving," and that we are not to be "anxious for the morrow; for the morrow will be anxious for itself." That is, it will bring its own proper load of labor and of care, from which you have no right to borrow for to-day's uses; which you cannot diminish by the same process.

George MacDonald puts this great principle aptly:

"You have a disagreeable duty to do at twelve o'clock. Do not blacken nine, and ten and eleven with the color of twelve. Do the work of each and reap your reward in peace."

One woman makes it her boast that she never sets bread for the morning that she does not lie awake half the night wondering how it will "turn out." She is so besotted in her ignorance as to think that the useless folly proves her to be a person of exquisite sensibility, whereas it testifies to lack of self-control, common sense and economical instincts.

It was old John Newton who likened the appointed tasks and trials of men to so many logs of wood, each lettered with the name of the day of the week, and no single one of them too heavy to be borne by a mortal of ordinary strength. If we will persist; he went on to say, in adding Tuesday's stick to Monday's, and Wednesday's and Thursday's and Friday's to that marked for Tuesday, "it is small wonder that we sink beneath the burden."

Our Heavenly Father would have us carry one stick at a time, and for this task has regulated our systems—mental, moral and spiritual. We, like the presumptuous bunglers that we are, bind the sticks into faggots, and then whine because our strength gives out.

The lesson of unlearning what we have practiced so long is not easy, but it may be acquired. In your character as day laborer, sift carefully each morning what belongs to to-day from that which may come to-morrow. Be rigid with yourself in this adjustment. If you find the weight beginning to tell upon bodily or mental muscles, ask your reason, as well as your conscience, whether or not the strain may not be from to-morrow's log.

For example: You have a servant who suits you, and whom you had hoped you suited. She is quiet to-day, with a pre-occupied look in her eye that may mean CHANGE.

As a housekeeper you will sustain me in the assertion that the portent suffices to send the thermometer of your spirits down to "twenty above," if not "ten below." Instead of brooding over the train of discomforts that would attend upon the threatened exodus, bethink yourself that since Norah cannot go without a week's warning you have nothing to-day to do with possibilities of a morrow that is seven times removed, *and put the thing out of your mind.*

In the italicized passage lies the secret of a tranquil soul. Learn by degrees to acquire power over your own imagination. By-and-by you will be surprised to find that you have formed a habit of reining it when it would presage disaster. It is not getting ready for house-cleaning to-day that terrifies you so much as the fancy that with the morrow will begin the actual scrubbing and window-washing. You do not mind ripping up an old gown while John reads to you under the evening lamp, but you are positively cross in the reflection that you must sew all of to-morrow with the seamstress who is to put the gown together again.

I may have told elsewhere the anecdote of the pious negro who was asked what he would do if the Lord were to order him to jump through a stone wall.

"I'd gird up my lines (loins) an' go at it!" said Sam, stoutly. "Goin' *at* it is my business; puttin' me *troo* is de Lord's!"

The story is good enough to be repeated and called to mind many times during the day, which is absolutely all of life with which we have to do.

Try the principle—and the practice—recommended in this simple heart-to-heart talk, dear sister. The habit of living by the day, rooted in faith in Him who guarantees grace for that time, and pledges no more, is better than the philosopher's stone. The peace it brings is deep-seated and abides, for it is founded upon a sure mercy and a certain promise.

FAREWELL!

Choose from Thousands of 1stWorldLibrary Classics By

A. M. Barnard
Ada Leverson
Adolphus William Ward
Aesop
Agatha Christie
Alexander Aaronsohn
Alexander Kielland
Alexandre Dumas
Alfred Gatty
Alfred Ollivant
Alice Duer Miller
Alice Turner Curtis
Alice Dunbar
Allen Chapman
Alleyne Ireland
Ambrose Bierce
Amelia E. Barr
Amory H. Bradford
Andrew Lang
Andrew McFarland Davis
Andy Adams
Angela Brazil
Anna Alice Chapin
Anna Sewell
Annie Besant
Annie Hamilton Donnell
Annie Payson Call
Annie Roe Carr
Annonaymous
Anton Chekhov
Archibald Lee Fletcher
Arnold Bennett
Arthur C. Benson
Arthur Conan Doyle
Arthur M. Winfield
Arthur Ransome
Arthur Schnitzler
Arthur Train
Atticus
B.H. Baden-Powell
B. M. Bower
B. C. Chatterjee
Baroness Emmuska Orczy
Baroness Orczy
Basil King
Bayard Taylor
Ben Macomber
Bertha Muzzy Bower
Bjornstjerne Bjornson

Booth Tarkington
Boyd Cable
Bram Stoker
C. Collodi
C. E. Orr
C. M. Ingleby
Carolyn Wells
Catherine Parr Traill
Charles A. Eastman
Charles Amory Beach
Charles Dickens
Charles Dudley Warner
Charles Farrar Browne
Charles Ives
Charles Kingsley
Charles Klein
Charles Hanson Towne
Charles Lathrop Pack
Charles Romyn Dake
Charles Whibley
Charles Willing Beale
Charlotte M. Braeme
Charlotte M. Yonge
Charlotte Perkins Stetson
Clair W. Hayes
Clarence Day Jr.
Clarence E. Mulford
Clemence Housman
Confucius
Coningsby Dawson
Cornelis DeWitt Wilcox
Cyril Burleigh
D. H. Lawrence
Daniel Defoe
David Garnett
Dinah Craik
Don Carlos Janes
Donald Keyhoe
Dorothy Kilner
Dougan Clark
Douglas Fairbanks
E. Nesbit
E. P. Roe
E. Phillips Oppenheim
E. S. Brooks
Earl Barnes
Edgar Rice Burroughs
Edith Van Dyne
Edith Wharton

Edward Everett Hale
Edward J. O'Biren
Edward S. Ellis
Edwin L. Arnold
Eleanor Atkins
Eleanor Hallowell Abbott
Eliot Gregory
Elizabeth Gaskell
Elizabeth McCracken
Elizabeth Von Arnim
Ellem Key
Emerson Hough
Emilie F. Carlen
Emily Bronte
Emily Dickinson
Enid Bagnold
Enilor Macartney Lane
Erasmus W. Jones
Ernie Howard Pie
Ethel May Dell
Ethel Turner
Ethel Watts Mumford
Eugene Sue
Eugenie Foa
Eugene Wood
Eustace Hale Ball
Evelyn Everett-green
Everard Cotes
F. H. Cheley
F. J. Cross
F. Marion Crawford
Fannie E. Newberry
Federick Austin Ogg
Ferdinand Ossendowski
Fergus Hume
Florence A. Kilpatrick
Fremont B. Deering
Francis Bacon
Francis Darwin
Frances Hodgson Burnett
Frances Parkinson Keyes
Frank Gee Patchin
Frank Harris
Frank Jewett Mather
Frank L. Packard
Frank V. Webster
Frederic Stewart Isham
Frederick Trevor Hill
Frederick Winslow Taylor

Friedrich Kerst	Hayden Carruth	James Branch Cabell
Friedrich Nietzsche	Helent Hunt Jackson	James DeMille
Fyodor Dostoyevsky	Helen Nicolay	James Joyce
G.A. Henty	Hendrik Conscience	James Lane Allen
G.K. Chesterton	Hendy David Thoreau	James Lane Allen
Gabrielle E. Jackson	Henri Barbusse	James Oliver Curwood
Garrett P. Serviss	Henrik Ibsen	James Oppenheim
Gaston Leroux	Henry Adams	James Otis
George A. Warren	Henry Ford	James R. Driscoll
George Ade	Henry Frost	Jane Abbott
Geroge Bernard Shaw	Henry James	Jane Austen
George Cary Eggleston	Henry Jones Ford	Jane L. Stewart
George Durston	Henry Seton Merriman	Janet Aldridge
George Ebers	Henry W Longfellow	Jens Peter Jacobsen
George Eliot	Herbert A. Giles	Jerome K. Jerome
George Gissing	Herbert Carter	Jessie Graham Flower
George MacDonald	Herbert N. Casson	John Buchan
George Meredith	Herman Hesse	John Burroughs
George Orwell	Hildegard G. Frey	John Cournos
George Sylvester Viereck	Homer	John F. Kennedy
George Tucker	Honore De Balzac	John Gay
George W. Cable	Horace B. Day	John Glasworthy
George Wharton James	Horace Walpole	John Habberton
Gertrude Atherton	Horatio Alger Jr.	John Joy Bell
Gordon Casserly	Howard Pyle	John Kendrick Bangs
Grace E. King	Howard R. Garis	John Milton
Grace Gallatin	Hugh Lofting	John Philip Sousa
Grace Greenwood	Hugh Walpole	John Taintor Foote
Grant Allen	Humphry Ward	Jonas Lauritz Idemil Lie
Guillermo A. Sherwell	Ian Maclaren	Jonathan Swift
Gulielma Zollinger	Inez Haynes Gillmore	Joseph A. Altsheler
Gustav Flaubert	Irving Bacheller	Joseph Carey
H. A. Cody	Isabel Cecilia Williams	Joseph Conrad
H. B. Irving	Isabel Hornibrook	Joseph E. Badger Jr
H.C. Bailey	Israel Abrahams	Joseph Hergesheimer
H. G. Wells	Ivan Turgenev	Joseph Jacobs
H. H. Munro	J.G.Austin	Jules Vernes
H. Irving Hancock	J. Henri Fabre	Julian Hawthrone
H. R. Naylor	J. M. Barrie	Julie A Lippmann
H. Rider Haggard	J. M. Walsh	Justin Huntly McCarthy
H. W. C. Davis	J. Macdonald Oxley	Kakuzo Okakura
Haldeman Julius	J. R. Miller	Karle Wilson Baker
Hall Caine	J. S. Fletcher	Kate Chopin
Hamilton Wright Mabie	J. S. Knowles	Kenneth Grahame
Hans Christian Andersen	J. Storer Clouston	Kenneth McGaffey
Harold Avery	J. W. Duffield	Kate Langley Bosher
Harold McGrath	Jack London	Kate Langley Bosher
Harriet Beecher Stowe	Jacob Abbott	Katherine Cecil Thurston
Harry Castlemon	James Allen	Katherine Stokes
Harry Coghill	James Andrews	L. A. Abbot
Harry Houidini	James Baldwin	L. T. Meade

L. Frank Baum
Latta Griswold
Laura Dent Crane
Laura Lee Hope
Laurence Housman
Lawrence Beasley
Leo Tolstoy
Leonid Andreyev
Lewis Carroll
Lewis Sperry Chafer
Lilian Bell
Lloyd Osbourne
Louis Hughes
Louis Joseph Vance
Louis Tracy
Louisa May Alcott
Lucy Fitch Perkins
Lucy Maud Montgomery
Luther Benson
Lydia Miller Middleton
Lyndon Orr
M. Corvus
M. H. Adams
Margaret E. Sangster
Margret Howth
Margaret Vandercook
Margaret W. Hungerford
Margret Penrose
Maria Edgeworth
Maria Thompson Daviess
Mariano Azuela
Marion Polk Angellotti
Mark Overton
Mark Twain
Mary Austin
Mary Catherine Crowley
Mary Cole
Mary Hastings Bradley
Mary Roberts Rinehart
Mary Rowlandson
M. Wollstonecraft Shelley
Maud Lindsay
Max Beerbohm
Myra Kelly
Nathaniel Hawthrone
Nicolo Machiavelli
O. F. Walton
Oscar Wilde

Owen Johnson
P.G. Wodehouse
Paul and Mabel Thorne
Paul G. Tomlinson
Paul Severing
Percy Brebner
Percy Keese Fitzhugh
Peter B. Kyne
Plato
Quincy Allen
R. Derby Holmes
R. L. Stevenson
R. S. Ball
Rabindranath Tagore
Rahul Alvares
Ralph Bonehill
Ralph Henry Barbour
Ralph Victor
Ralph Waldo Emmerson
Rene Descartes
Ray Cummings
Rex Beach
Rex E. Beach
Richard Harding Davis
Richard Jefferies
Richard Le Gallienne
Robert Barr
Robert Frost
Robert Gordon Anderson
Robert L. Drake
Robert Lansing
Robert Lynd
Robert Michael Ballantyne
Robert W. Chambers
Rosa Nouchette Carey
Rudyard Kipling
Saint Augustine
Samuel B. Allison
Samuel Hopkins Adams
Sarah Bernhardt
Sarah C. Hallowell
Selma Lagerlof
Sherwood Anderson
Sigmund Freud
Standish O'Grady
Stanley Weyman
Stella Benson
Stella M. Francis

Stephen Crane
Stewart Edward White
Stijn Streuvels
Swami Abhedananda
Swami Parmananda
T. S. Ackland
T. S. Arthur
The Princess Der Ling
Thomas A. Janvier
Thomas A Kempis
Thomas Anderton
Thomas Bailey Aldrich
Thomas Bulfinch
Thomas De Quincey
Thomas Dixon
Thomas H. Huxley
Thomas Hardy
Thomas More
Thornton W. Burgess
U. S. Grant
Upton Sinclair
Valentine Williams
Various Authors
Vaughan Kester
Victor Appleton
Victor G. Durham
Victoria Cross
Virginia Woolf
Wadsworth Camp
Walter Camp
Walter Scott
Washington Irving
Wilbur Lawton
Wilkie Collins
Willa Cather
Willard F. Baker
William Dean Howells
William le Queux
W. Makepeace Thackeray
William W. Walter
William Shakespeare
Winston Churchill
Yei Theodora Ozaki
Yogi Ramacharaka
Young E. Allison
Zane Grey

www.ingramcontent.com/pod-product-compliance
Lightning Source LLC
Chambersburg PA
CBHW030127180626
46812CB00002B/592